# The Mediterranean Diet for Beginners

# The Mediterranean Diet for Beginners

110 Delicious Recipes and the Complete Guide to Going Mediterranean

By Lauren Mcdonnell

# Table of Contents

# Introduction

The term "diet" for most of us spells out deprivation, extreme hunger, and bland and boring foods that we are forced to eat in order to lose weight. However, with the Mediterranean diet, none of those apply.

The Mediterranean diet is endowed with an unlimited assortment of fresh, healthy, natural, and wholesome foods from all food groups. Although there is a greater focus on certain ingredients, no natural ingredients are excluded.

Mediterranean diet devotees are able to enjoy their favorite dishes as they learn to appreciate how nourishing the freshest healthy and natural foods can be.

This diet is primarily based on the eating habits of the original inhabitants of the coasts of Greece, Italy, Spain, Morocco, and France. Because of their temperate climate and location, seasonal fresh fruit, vegetables, and seafood form the nutritional foundation of these regions.

The simplest way to understand the Mediterranean diet is to picture eating as though it's summer every day. It might also give you a déjà vu moment by reminding you of the foods you enjoyed most on a summer vacation or at the beach. In truth, there is never a dull moment with the Mediterranean diet!

All fun aside, the Mediterranean diet will help you find great pleasure in food, knowing that every bite you take is going to provide your body with the healthiest nutrition.

When your food tastes like you are on a perpetual vacation, it's easy and exciting to stay on the bandwagon!

# Understanding the Mediterranean Diet

Unless you've been living under a rock, you have definitely heard of the Mediterranean diet. This diet has received a lot of press over the last couple of years, and all for the right reasons. Also known as the heart-healthy diet, the Mediterranean diet is considered to be the most nutritious and most realistic diet on the planet.

## The Mediterranean diet unchained

If we take an in-depth look at the Mediterranean diet, it's not really a *diet* per se, as in the sense of being a weight-loss tool—it's more of a lifestyle and a culinary tradition for the people of the Mediterranean region. Its main focus is on whole grains, fresh fruit and vegetables, seafood, nuts, olive oil, and a glass of wine every now and then.

The Mediterranean diet is part of a culture that appreciates the freshest ingredients, prepared in a simple but tasty way and shared with friends and family in a laid-back environment.

Most of us understand the importance of eating a clean and well-balanced diet for improved health and better quality of life, but very few of us actually put this into practice. With most of us spending a greater percentage of our days at work, we tend to opt for fast and easy options when it comes to the food we eat. In fact, in many cases fast food, frozen dinners from food stores, and processed foods are our first options.

Over the years, people across the globe have stopped eating seasonal foods because we can now access all kinds of food, all year round. What's more, cooking meals from scratch seems to be an unnecessary hassle, considering our overburdened schedules and the time it takes to make a good meal.

As a result, we are eating foods that are made in a plant instead of food that grows as a plant. Our diets are characterized by over-processed foods, unhealthy fats, truckloads of sugar, and lots and lots of artificial ingredients, the names of which most of us can't even pronounce.

Perhaps one of the greatest attributes of the Mediterranean diet is the fact that it is very simple and straightforward. You don't need to be a celebrity chef to make the tastiest meals, as you will find out in our recipes section. Eat less red meat and instead eat more fish—especially fatty fish that are rich in omega-3 fatty acids—cook with extra virgin olive oil, and eat fresh fruit, vegetables, whole grains and nuts several times a day.

Unlike many popular diets, many of which are fads, the Mediterranean diet encourages consumption of healthy fats from olive oil, fish, avocado, nuts and seeds. Additionally, the occasional glass of red wine can help lower your risk of cardiovascular disease.

For a quick round-up of the Mediterranean diet:

- **Eat a plant-centered diet**

You should build your meals around fresh and organic fruits, vegetables, legumes, nuts and beans. These whole foods will provide your body with top-grade nutrition in the form of fiber-rich complex carbs that are slow digesting, as well as antioxidants, vitamins, and phytochemicals.

Additionally, these foods will keep you full longer, due to their high fiber content, and thus will help keep you from snacking on unhealthy food, while providing you with disease-fighting nutrition at the same time.

- **Only eat whole grains**

Avoid refined grain products such as white rice and bleached white flour, which have been stripped of most of their healthful nutrients. Instead, go for whole grain products such as oats, brown rice, whole wheat, bulgur, farro, barley, quinoa, millet corn, and so on. Whole grains are higher in fiber, minerals and vitamins.

- **Eat fish or shellfish at least two times in a week**

Fish and shellfish are very low in saturated fat, and they provide your body with essential omega-3 fatty acids. Popular fish and shellfish in the Mediterranean diet include: clams, anchovies, salmon, mussels, bream, octopus, sardines, shrimp, herring, crab, squid, tuna and sea bass.

However, make sure you only source wild-caught fish, to avoid the mercury contamination common in farmed fish.

- **Eat small portions of red meat every once in a while**

Red meat is very high in saturated fat. While we include it in the Mediterranean diet for its health benefits, you should eat it in moderation.

- **Eat as little dairy as possible and limit it to cheese and yogurt**

Cheese and natural yogurt, when consumed in moderation, are a very healthy part of the Mediterranean diet. These ensure you get enough calcium to promote healthy bones. Yogurt also supplies your body with probiotics that aid digestion by populating your gut with healthy bacteria.

- **Get your healthy fats from olives, avocado, fatty fish, nuts, seeds and olive oil**

Olives and olive oil in general are rich in monounsaturated fats and antioxidants that promote heart health. Eat olives as a snack or add them to stews, salads, or pasta dishes. Avocado is also rich in unsaturated fats. You can eat it as-is, or use it in a smoothie or salad.

Nuts and seeds such as almonds, walnuts, hazelnuts, cashews, pine nuts, sesame seeds, and pumpkin seeds are all good sources of healthy fats.

Avoid saturated fats found in cream, butter, lard, and red meat, as well as trans fats that are found in margarine or hydrogenated oils.

- **Drink an occasional glass of red wine**

When taken in moderation, red wine may improve your heart's health by boosting the levels of good cholesterol (HDL), which can be attributed to special antioxidants found in red wine.

- **It's all about moderation**

Though no food is strictly off limits, it's important to watch what you are eating, as well as your portion sizes, especially when eating foods containing high levels of saturated fat and high-calorie foods. Try as much as possible to eat natural and wholesome food for improved health.

- **Take time to be physically active and enjoy life**

The Mediterranean lifestyle is more relaxed compared to the typical western lifestyle. People in the Mediterranean region take their time to enjoy meals with friends and family. Most walk or ride a bike to work instead of driving, and they take more vacations, thereby reducing stress.

## Where it all began – The history of Mediterranean eating

The Mediterranean tradition is characterized by a cuisine rich in aromas, colors, and beautiful memories that support the spirit—and taste—of those who are in tune with nature.

For some time now, everyone has been talking about the Mediterranean diet, but only a handful of people follow it properly. For some, the Mediterranean diet is all about pizza, and for others, it's pasta and meat sauce. In this book, we are going to have a look at its beginnings to have a better sense of exactly what the Mediterranean diet entails.

This heart-healthy diet has its origins in the Mediterranean basin, commonly referred to as "The Cradle of Society" because the whole history of the ancient world took place within its geographical borders.

The true origins of the Mediterranean diet are, however, lost in time. We might look back to the eating habits and patterns of the Middle Ages, or even further, to the Roman culture (which modeled the Greek culture), and their identification of red wine, bread and oil as symbols of their rural culture.

Many people in the Mediterranean region farmed the land and produced fruits and vegetables; they also fished for food. Beef and dairy were not very common in this region, as the climate is not ideal for grazing. Fish, goats, and lamb were the most common protein sources.

# The science behind the Mediterranean diet

There is a reason why the Mediterranean diet is often referred to as the "heart-healthy diet." This diet is traditionally high in fresh fruit and vegetables, cereals, and legumes, with moderate consumption of fatty fish and dairy, and a limited consumption of meat, saturated fat and sugar.

Most of the fat found in this diet comes from olive oil, avocado, fish, nuts, and seeds. Alcohol is consumed in moderation in the form of red wine.

Scientific research carried out in the 1960s showed that men who adhered to a traditional Mediterranean diet had lower incidences of heart attacks, hence the origin of the "heart-healthy" diet.

Additional investigations have shown that the Mediterranean diet is linked to lower incidences of stroke, cardiovascular disease, type 2 diabetes, and untimely deaths from health issues. Adherence to the principles of the Mediterranean diet has also been shown to improve cognitive ability.

A systemic review carried out to determine the effect of the Mediterranean diet on dementia showed positive results. The Mediterranean diet offers high levels of antioxidants from the intake of fresh fruit and vegetables as well as occasional glass of red wine. These antioxidants may help protect against damage to brain cells associated with Alzheimer's disease, and also increase the levels of protein in your brain that protect your brain cells from damage.

Inflammation is the main culprit behind Alzheimer's disease, and the Mediterranean diet is an effective anti-inflammatory diet. For many of us, the Mediterranean diet is the greatest health insurance policy we can take to guarantee great health!

# Discover Health and Longevity on the Mediterranean Diet

Eating a Mediterranean diet is definitely one of the keys to the fountain of youth, thanks to its fresh, healthy, natural, nutritious, and wholesome food profile. Embark on this diet as soon as possible, and you will start noticing distinct improvements in your appearance as well as energy levels. Start eating the Mediterranean diet now for better health later.

## Why should you be eating the Mediterranean diet?

- **Low in processed foods and artificial sugars**

The Mediterranean diet is made up of foods that are very close to their naturally occurring state, like olive oil, peas, legumes, fruits, nuts, seeds, vegetables, and unrefined whole grain products. Beyond plant-based foods, another common food is wild-caught fish, with sardines, salmon, and anchovies being the most popular options. A moderate consumption of goat, cow or sheep cheeses and yogurts is encouraged as a way of receiving calcium, healthy fats, and good cholesterol.

While most people in the Mediterranean region are not vegetarian, this diet promotes a very small consumption of meat. Choose healthier options that will improve your health and also help you lose weight.

- **Healthy and sustainable weight loss**

If you are looking to shed excess pounds without feeling deprived, and keep the weight off for the rest of your life, this is the plan for you. This diet has been undertaken by numerous people with great success, not just in weight loss, but overall health, as it naturally eliminates processed foods and unhealthy fats by putting more focus on plant-based foods.

Additionally, there's room for interpretation in the Mediterranean diet, whether you prefer to eat a low-protein diet, or a low-carb diet, or a diet that's in between. The main focus of the Mediterranean diet is on the consumption of fruits, vegetables, healthy fat and high-quality protein.

- **Improves your heart health**

Olive oil plays an important role in the Mediterranean diet. Alpha-linoleic acid is a compound found in olive oil, and has been shown to reduce the risk of deaths related to cardiac problems by up to 45 percent.

An adherence to the Mediterranean diet, which includes omega-3 and monounsaturated fats, has been shown to reduce mortality linked to heart disease, as it lowers high blood pressure as well as bad cholesterol levels.

- **Fights off cancer**

The Mediterranean diet offers a balanced ratio between omega-3 and omega-6 essential fats, as well as a healthy supply of fiber, vitamins, antioxidants, minerals, and polyphenols that are found in olive oil, fruit, vegetables, and wine.

This antioxidant-rich diet helps fight cancer right, left and center, by protecting your DNA from damage, lowering inflammation, stopping cell mutation and delaying the growth of tumors.

Olive oil has also been shown to reduce the risk of bowel and colon cancers.

- **Prevents and reduces symptoms of diabetes**

The Mediterranean diet is the ultimate anti-inflammatory diet, thanks to its emphasis on organic and natural produce. This anti-inflammatory property helps fight chronic diseases associated with chronic inflammation, such as type 2 diabetes.

The Mediterranean diet keeps diabetes at bay by regulating your insulin levels. An excess of insulin, the hormone that controls your blood sugar levels, makes you gain weight and store sugar and other carbohydrates as fat.

When you regulate your blood sugar levels using a healthy diet, your body becomes more efficient at burning fat. This helps you stabilize blood sugar levels, and can also help you lose weight.

- **Improves mood and boosts cognitive function**

This heart-healthy diet is a natural way to preserve your memory, and when followed keenly, might help prevent and reduce symptoms of Parkinson's disease, dementia and Alzheimer's disease. Problems occur when your brain does not receive adequate nutrition to help in the synthesis of dopamine, a hormone that's responsible for mood regulation, proper body movement and thought processing.

The healthy nutrition provided by the Mediterranean diet fights off the harmful effects of exposure to toxins, and also helps prevent age-related cognitive decline.

- **Longevity**

A fresh, healthy, natural, organic, and wholesome diet means that every system in your body will be operating at optimal capacity, thus giving you newfound energy to carry on with your daily responsibilities. Your skin will improve, your hair will improve. Everything about you will be as good as new!

- **A great de-stressor and relaxant**

The Mediterranean lifestyle is not confined to what you eat; it encourages you to spend quality time with nature and the people you love, such as your family and friends. There's no greater way to have fun with your family than over a delicious and healthy home-cooked meal served outdoors, as you crack jokes and do what you all love to do. Maybe even dance!

Nothing beats a glass of red wine after a meal shared with family.

The Mediterranean diet is a way of life that will improve your overall health, help you lose weight and find balance in life. It will teach you how to have a deep appreciation for nature and all that it has to offer.

## The Tastiest Path to Weight Loss

Start taking advantage of the season's abundant produce and enjoy this heart-healthy diet rich in antioxidants, unsaturated fats, vitamins, and minerals. You can even fire up your grill on this weight-loss journey, as you enjoy the tastiest dishes and a slimmer you, Mediterranean style!

- **Fruits and vegetables—energy to keep off junk food**

If you are running low on antioxidants, phytochemicals, and micro-nutrients such as vitamins and minerals, you are not going to lose weight! Scientific research has shown that we are more likely to eat junk food when feeling fatigued, but the micro-nutrients in fruits and vegetables rev up your metabolism and provide your body with clean and first-class energy.

Additionally, dehydration is oftentimes confused with hunger. You might find yourself munching on the nearest snack, when all you needed was a refreshing glass of water. Most vegetables average around 90 percent water, thus helping prevent even the mildest form of dehydration that can slow down your body's fat-burning ability.

- **Olive oil—its scent alone sets off your body's fat-burning process!**

Extra virgin olive oil contains the highest percentage of monounsaturated fat compared to other foods and oils. By reducing the amount of saturated fats you consume and increasing your intake of olive oil, the first thing you are going to notice is increased energy levels. You are also going to burn off more fat to keep your energy levels high.

Additionally, you can curb your appetite before your meals by smelling olive oil. Apply olive oil on your bread in place of butter, and use it in your salads and cooking for faster, sustainable weight loss.

- **Natural Greek yogurt—the right bacteria to burn fat**

This yogurt has more protein per ounce compared to any other ready-to-eat food. As a result, it helps keep you full longer, reduce cravings, and keep your blood sugar levels stable, and it also prevents overeating.

Additionally, your body uses more energy to metabolize protein, compared to carbs. Greek yogurt is also endowed with healthy probiotics that populate your gut with friendly bacteria to fight off bacteria, germs, viruses, and disease.

- **Legumes—both types of fiber needed to lose weight**

Soluble and insoluble fiber are very important for weight loss. No single food on the planet has more of a combination of the two than legumes.

Soluble fiber dissolves in the liquids in your gut to form a gel-like solution. This expands to make you feel fuller, and it also holds on longer to the foods in your stomach, thus slowing down the digestive process.

Insoluble fiber, on the other hand, absorbs water and adds bulk to your digestive tract. This slowing down of the digestive process means you won't get the urge to snack on junk food.

- **Seafood—adds fire to the fat-burning process**

Today, more Americans do not meet their omega-3 fatty acid requirements essential to blood sugar sensitivity, metabolism, and any other system involved in the body's fat-burning process.

Coldwater fatty fish such as salmon, herring, and sardines have more omega-3 fatty acids than leaner fish. Seafood as a whole contains EPA/ DHA omega-3 fats, the most potent omega-3 fatty acids.

Eating fish and shellfish as per the Mediterranean diet's recommendations will increase your metabolism by up to 400 calories a day, and also prevent your fat cells from growing, especially around your tummy area.

# Embarking on the Mediterranean Diet

So far, we are clear on the fact that the Mediterranean diet is not a fad diet with a catchy title that will make you lose ten pounds in one week. In very simple terms, it's a common-sense approach to food and living that will improve your health, quality of life, and general well-being.

One reason why this diet is very practical and easy to follow is the fact that it does not ban any major food groups. In addition, it is not an expensive diet to maintain. Let us now look at an easy approach to start following this heart-healthy diet.

## Failure to plan is planning to fail

There are small things you can do that will change your life forever, and they start with having a clear plan that involves setting goals. However, setting your goals is often the easiest part—it's achieving them that can be a bit of a challenge.

The best way to achieve your goals is to make them into a science: plan, plan and plan. Start with plan A and if it doesn't work, move to plan B and so on, but no matter what, never quit!

- **Take it one step at a time**

Take baby steps and focus on one goal at a time. Start with a goal that you are confident you can do every day for the next week: like getting up when your alarm rings without having to use the snooze button, or eating fresh vegetables at every meal.

Being successful doesn't only mean an achievement, it means you have picked up a new healthy habit. Once you have acquired one, what's to stop you from acquiring more healthy habits?

- **Be driven by deadlines, and always write them down**

Having deadlines will turn your "I wish" into "I did it!"

Writing down each deadline gives life to your goals, and is a very powerful way of making a commitment to yourself.

You now know the principles of the Mediterranean diet. Add a sustainable exercise regimen to these, and you will be on your path to great health.

Remember to take it one day at a time, and eventually, the Mediterranean diet will be second nature to you.

# 8 Top tips for success

## 1. Compare the Mediterranean diet pyramid with the USDA food pyramid

The Mediterranean diet gives greater emphasis to fruits, vegetables, legumes, whole grains, olive oil, and natural herbs and spices; eating fish and shellfish a couple of times a week; and enjoying eggs, poultry, cheese, yogurt, red meat, and wine in moderation.

When compared to the USDA's food pyramid, the Mediterranean diet pyramid has smaller amounts of red meat, sweet fruits, and dairy, and instead allows for a greater intake of healthy fats and oils.

## 2. Eat breakfast every day, no matter how busy your schedule

By now you know that breakfast is your most important meal of the day. It breaks the all-night fast, hence the term "breakfast," coined from "break the fast." A nutrient-rich breakfast—packed with fruits, vegetables, whole grains, and other fiber-rich foods—will boost your energy levels for the day and keep you full until your next meal.

## 3. Know the difference between healthy and unhealthy fats

Monounsaturated fats are healthy fats are found in olives, sunflower seeds, avocados, extra virgin olive oil and nuts.

Polyunsaturated oils, also healthy fats, are found in soybean, sunflower, corn, and safflower oils. These promote heart health and also lower bad cholesterol levels.

Saturated fats and trans fats, on the other hand, are considered unhealthy fats, and overconsumption can increase your risk of cardiovascular illnesses and also elevate your bad cholesterol levels.

### 4. Eat as many vegetables as possible in every meal

Vegetables are rich in fiber, which helps keep you full longer and also boosts digestion. Load up your sandwiches, soups, omelets, stews, pizza, and any other meal with fresh vegetables, herbs, and spices.

### 5. Reduce your meat intake

Did you know that Americans eat more meat than any other nation in the world? This might partly explain why we are one of the fattest countries, if not *the* fattest.

By reducing your red meat intake, you will also be reducing your intake of saturated and trans fats found in meat products.

You can occasionally have red meat, but it should be in small portions and from lean cuts.

### 6. Eat fish and seafood twice a week

Fish such as salmon, tuna, sardines, and herring are rich in omega-3 fatty acids. Shellfish such as oysters, mussels, and clams have healthy benefits for your brain and heart. Keep meals interesting by trying out new recipes like the ones we are going to share in our recipes section.

### 7. Sit down to family meals on a regular basis

The Mediterranean diet has its foundation in cultures having a pleasant time at mealtime, with family and friends sharing tasty and healthy food and drinks.

For most of us, our overburdened schedules make it very difficult to have a family meal, where we can all eat and make merry. However, this is not just important for your health, but for your family as well. Eating companionably together tightens your family bond as you savor nutritious food.

### 8. Keep fit

Regardless of how busy you are, make some time to play with your kids, go for a walk around your block, or go to the gym, or to dancing lessons. Whatever your fitness preference. JUST DO IT! You should commit to getting at least 30 minutes of exercise on a regular basis.

Get off your desk chair or your couch and get moving for a healthier body.

# Eating on the Mediterranean Diet

There is no one "right" way to do the Mediterranean diet. The fact that there are many countries in the Mediterranean region, with people who don't eat the same things, is enough to show that there is "no one size fits all" technique to this diet.

## Exactly what's on your plate?

The key is to ensure that your plate is always filled with plant-based foods, with fruits and vegetables taking the biggest portion. Eat fish 2-3 times in a week, and occasionally eat red meat. Whole grains and legumes should also feature on your plate, as they are very nutritious. Nuts and seeds make a great snack—and of course, don't forget to cook your food in olive oil.

Water is the ultimate Mediterranean diet drink—you should take at least eight glasses of water every day. A glass of red wine to go with your dinner will also do your heart some good!

## A simplified Mediterranean diet shopping guide

You should always choose the least processed foods, with a higher priority being on fresh and organic produce. It's advisable to shop around the perimeter of the grocery store: This is usually where whole foods are found.

Here is a simple list you can use the next time you go food shopping:

- Fruits: grapes, apples, berries, citrus fruits, avocado, bananas, papaya, pineapple, etc.
- Vegetables: broccoli, mushrooms, celery, carrots, kale, onions, leeks, eggplant, etc.
- Frozen vegetables: healthy mixed veggie options
- Legumes: beans, lentils, peas, etc.
- Grains: all whole grains including whole-grain pasta and whole-grain bread
- Nuts: almonds, walnuts, cashews, hazelnuts, pistachios, pine nuts, etc.
- Seeds: pumpkin, hemp, sesame, sunflower, etc.
- Fish: salmon, tuna, herring, sardines, sea bass, etc.
- Shellfish varieties and shrimp

- Free-range chicken
- Baby potatoes and sweet potatoes
- Cheese
- Natural Greek yogurt
- Olives
- Pastured eggs
- Meat: goat, pork, and pastured beef
- Extra virgin olive oil

As a rule of thumb, eliminate all unhealthy foods not supported by the Mediterranean diet from your kitchen, including candy, refined grain products, sodas and artificially sweetened beverages, crackers, and all other processed foods.

If the only food you have in your home is healthy, that is what you are going to eat. You can't eat what's not there!

## Tips for eating out on the Mediterranean diet

It's very easy to follow the Mediterranean diet when eating out.
- Have fish or seafood as your main dish
- Ask the chef to fry all your vegetables and food in extra virgin olive oil
- Eat whole-grain bread dipped in extra virgin olive oil instead of butter
- Have a glass of red wine, with fruits such as berries or grapes for dessert

Now that we understand all the principles of the Mediterranean diet, it's time for the best part: FOOD! Get your apron ready and let's get cooking!

# Mediterranean Breakfast Recipes

## Creamy Paninis

Total time: 15 minutes
Prep time: 10 minutes
Cook time: 5 minutes
Yield: 4 servings

### Ingredients
- 2 tbsp. finely chopped black olives, oil-cured
- ¼ cup chopped fresh basil leaves
- ½ cup mayonnaise dressing with Olive Oil, divided
- 8 slices whole-wheat bread
- 4 slices of bacon
- 1 small zucchini, thinly sliced
- 4 slices provolone cheese
- 7 oz. roasted red peppers, sliced

### Directions
- In a small bowl, combine olives, basil, and ¼ cup of mayonnaise; evenly spread the mayonnaise mixture on the bread slices and layer 4 slices with bacon, zucchini, provolone and peppers.
- Top with the remaining bread slices and spread the remaining ¼ cup of mayonnaise on the outside of the sandwiches; cook over medium heat for about 4 minutes, turning once, until cheese is melted and the sandwiches are golden brown.

# Breakfast Couscous

Total time: 15 minutes
Prep time: 10 minutes
Cook time: 5 minutes
Yield: 4 servings

## Ingredients
- 1 (2-inch) cinnamon stick
- 3 cups 1% low-fat milk
- 1 cup whole-wheat couscous (uncooked)
- 6 tsp. dark brown sugar, divided
- ¼ cup dried currants
- ½ cup chopped apricots (dried)
- ¼ tsp. sea salt
- 4 tsp. melted butter, divided

## Directions
- In a saucepan set over medium high heat, combine cinnamon stick and milk; heat for about 3 minutes (do not boil).
- Remove the pan from heat and stir in couscous, 4 teaspoons of sugar, currants, apricots, and sea salt. Let the mixture stand, covered, for at least 15 minutes.
- Discard the cinnamon stick and divide the couscous among four bowls; top each serving with ½ teaspoon of sugar and 1 teaspoon of melted butter.
- Serve immediately.

# Potato and Chickpea Hash

Total time: 15 minutes
Prep time: 10 minutes
Cook time: 5 minutes
Yield: 4 servings

## Ingredients
- 4 cups shredded frozen hash brown potatoes
- 1 tbsp. freshly minced ginger
- ½ cup chopped onion
- 2 cups chopped baby spinach
- 1 tbsp. curry powder
- ½ tsp. sea salt
- ¼ cup extra virgin olive oil
- 1 cup chopped zucchini
- 1 (15-ounce) can chickpeas, rinsed
- 4 large eggs

## Directions
- In a large bowl, combine the potatoes, ginger, onion, spinach, curry powder, and sea salt.
- In a nonstick skillet set over medium high heat, heat extra virgin olive oil and add the potato mixture.
- Press the mixture into a layer and cook for about 5 minutes, without stirring, or until golden brown and crispy.
- Lower heat to medium low and fold in zucchini and chickpeas, breaking up the mixture until just combined.
- Stir briefly, press the mixture back into a layer, and make four wells.
- Break one egg into each indentation.
- Cook, covered, for about 5 minutes or until eggs are set.

# Avocado Toast

Total time: 10 minutes
Prep time: 10 minutes
Cook time: 0 minutes
Yield: 4 servings

## Ingredients
- 2 ripe avocados, peeled
- Squeeze of fresh lemon juice, to taste
- 2 tbsp. freshly chopped mint, plus extra to garnish
- Sea salt and black pepper, to taste
- 4 large slices rye bread
- 80 grams soft feta, crumbled

## Directions
- In a medium bowl, mash the avocado roughly with a fork; add lemon juice and mint and continue mashing until just combined.
- Season with black pepper and sea salt to taste.
- Grill or toast bread until golden.
- Spread about ¼ of the avocado mixture onto each slice of the toasted bread and top with feta.
- Garnish with extra mint and serve immediately.

# Mediterranean Pancakes

Total time: 50 minutes
Prep time: 30 minutes
Cook time: 20 minutes
Yield: 16 Pancakes

## Ingredients

- 1 cup old-fashioned oats
- ½ cup all-purpose flour
- 2 tbsp. flax seeds
- 1 tsp. baking soda
- ¼ tsp. sea salt
- 2 tbsp. extra virgin olive oil
- 2 large eggs
- 2 cups nonfat plain Greek yogurt
- 2 tbsp. raw honey
- Fresh fruit, syrup, or other toppings

## Directions

- In a blender, combine oats, flour, flax seeds, baking soda, and sea salt; blend for about 30 seconds.
- Add extra virgin olive oil, eggs, yogurt, and honey and continue pulsing until very smooth.
- Let the mixture stand for at least 20 minutes or until thick.
- Set a large nonstick skillet over medium heat and brush with extra virgin olive oil.
- In batches, ladle the batter by quarter-cupfuls into the skillet.
- Cook the pancakes for about 2 minutes or until bubbles form and golden brown.
- Turn them over and cook the other sides for 2 minutes more or until golden brown.
- Transfer the cooked pancakes to a baking sheet and keep warm in oven.
- Serve with favorite toppings.

# Mediterranean Frittata

Total time: 25 minutes
Prep time: 10 minutes
Cook time: 15 minutes
Yield: 4 servings

## Ingredients

- 3 tbsp. extra virgin olive oil, divided
- 1 cup chopped onion
- 2 cloves garlic, minced
- 8 eggs, beaten
- ¼ cup half-and-half, milk or light cream
- ½ cup sliced Kalamata olives
- ½ cup roasted red sweet peppers, chopped
- ½ cup crumbled feta cheese
- ⅛ tsp. black pepper
- ¼ cup fresh basil
- 2 tbsp. Parmesan cheese, finely shredded
- ½ cup coarsely crushed onion-and-garlic croutons
- Fresh basil leaves, to garnish

## Directions

- Preheat your broiler.
- Heat 2 tablespoons of extra virgin olive oil in a broiler-proof skillet set over medium heat; sauté onion and garlic for a few minutes or until tender.
- In the meantime, beat eggs and half-and-half in a bowl until well combined.
- Stir in olives, roasted sweet pepper, feta cheese, black pepper and basil.
- Pour the egg mixture over the sautéed onion mixture and cook until almost set.
- With a spatula, lift the egg mixture to allow the uncooked part to flow underneath.
- Continue cooking for 2 minutes more or until the set.
- Combine the remaining extra virgin olive oil, Parmesan cheese, and crushed croutons in a bowl; sprinkle the mixture over the frittata and broil for about 5 minutes or until the crumbs are golden and the top is set.
- To serve, cut the frittata into wedges and garnish with fresh basil.

# Nutty Banana Oatmeal

Total time: 15 minutes
Prep time: 10 minutes
Cook time: 5 minutes
Yield: 4 servings

## Ingredients
- ¼ cup quick cooking oats
- 3 tbsp. raw honey
- ½ cup skim milk
- 2 tbsp. chopped walnuts
- 1 tsp. flax seeds
- 1 banana, peeled

## Directions
- In a microwave-safe bowl, combine oats, honey, milk, walnuts, and flaxseeds; microwave on high for about 2 minutes.
- In a small bowl, mash the banana with a fork to a fine consistency; stir into the oatmeal and serve hot.

# Mediterranean Veggie Omelet

Total time: 40 minutes
Prep time: 15 minutes
Cook time: 25 minutes
Yield: 4 servings

## Ingredients
- 1 tbsp. extra virgin olive oil
- 2 cups thinly sliced fresh fennel bulb
- ¼ cup chopped artichoke hearts, soaked in water, drained
- ¼ cup pitted green olives, brine-cured, chopped
- 1 diced Roma tomato
- 6 eggs
- ¼ tsp. sea salt
- ½ tsp. freshly ground black pepper
- ½ cup goat cheese, crumbled
- 2 tbsp. freshly chopped fresh parsley, dill, or basil

## Directions
- Preheat your oven to 325°F.
- Heat extra virgin olive oil in an ovenproof skillet over medium heat.
- Sauté fennel for about 5 minutes or until tender.
- Add artichoke hearts, olives, and tomatoes and cook for 3minutes ore or until softened.
- In a bowl, beat the eggs; season with sea salt and pepper.
- Add the egg mixture over the vegetables and stir for about 2 minutes.
- Sprinkle cheese over the omelet and bake in the oven for about 5 minutes or until set and cooked through.
- Top with parsley, dill, or basil.
- Transfer the omelet onto a cutting board, carefully cut into four wedges, and serve immediately.

# Lemon Scones

Total time: 30 minutes
Prep time: 15 minutes
Cook time: 15 minutes
Yield: 12 servings

## Ingredients
- 2 cups plus ¼ cup flour
- ½ tsp. baking soda
- 2 tbsp. sugar
- ½ tsp. sea salt
- ¾ cup reduced-fat buttermilk
- Zest of 1 lemon
- 1 to 2 tsp. freshly squeezed lemon juice
- 1 cup powdered sugar

## Directions
- Preheat your oven to 400°F.
- In a food processor, combine 2 cups of flour, baking soda, sugar and salt until well blended.
- Add buttermilk and lemon zest and continue mixing to combine well.
- Sprinkle the remaining flour onto a clean surface and turn out the dough; gently knead the dough at least six times and shape it into a ball.
- Using a rolling pin, flatten the dough into half-inch thick circle.
- Cut the dough into four equal wedges and the cut each into three smaller wedges.
- Arrange the scones on a baking sheet and bake in preheated oven for about 15 minutes or until golden brown.
- Mix together lemon juice and the powdered sugar in a small bowl to make a thin frosting.
- Remove the scones from the oven and drizzle with lemon frosting while still hot.
- Serve right away.

# Breakfast Wrap

Total time: 10 minutes
Prep time: 5 minutes
Cooking time: 5 minutes
Yield: 2 servings

## Ingredients
- ½ cup fresh-picked spinach
- 4 egg whites
- 2 Bella sun-dried tomatoes
- 2 mixed-grain flax wraps
- ½ cup feta cheese crumbles

## Directions
- Cook spinach, egg whites and tomatoes in a frying pan for about 4 minutes or until lightly browned.
- Flip it over and cook the other side for 4 minutes or until almost done.
- Microwave the wraps for about 15 seconds; remove from the microwave, fill each wrap with the egg mixture, sprinkle with feta cheese crumbles and roll up.
- Cut each wrap into two parts and serve.

# Garlicky Scrambled Eggs

Total time: 25 minutes
Prep time: 10 minutes
Cooking time: 15 minutes
Yield: 2 servings

## Ingredients
- ½ tsp. extra virgin olive oil
- ½ cup ground beef
- ½ tsp. garlic powder
- 3 eggs
- Salt
- Pepper

## Directions
- Set a medium-sized pan over medium heat.
- Add extra virgin olive oil and heat until hot but not smoking.
- Stir in ground beef and cook for about 10 minutes or until almost done.
- Stir in garlic and sauté for about 2 minutes.
- In a large bowl, beat the eggs until almost frothy; season with salt and pepper.
- Add the egg mixture to the pan with the cooked beef and scramble until ready.
- Serve with toasted bread and olives, for a healthy, satisfying breakfast!

# Healthy Breakfast Casserole

Total time: 60 minutes
Prep time: 10 minutes
Cooking time: 50 minutes
Yield: 6 servings

## Ingredients
- 2 tbsp. extra virgin olive oil, divided
- ½ a medium-sized onion, diced
- 2 medium-sized yellow potatoes. diced
- 1 lb. zucchini, sliced
- 3 portabella mushroom caps, diced
- 150g torn fresh spinach
- 200g ricotta
- 200g light ricotta cheese
- 2 cups of egg whites
- 12 grape tomatoes, sliced into ⅓ pieces
- 3 peeled and roasted fresh peppers, sliced
- 2 sourdough rolls
- 4 tbsp. Pecorino Romano cheese, grated
- 100g skim-milk mozzarella cheese, grated

## Directions
- Preheat the oven to 400°F.
- Mix together olive oil, onion and potato and roast for at least 15 minutes; remove from oven and keep on the baking tray.
- In a bowl, combine together ½ tablespoon olive oil and zucchini; toss to coat well and transfer to a baking tray.
- Return all the vegetables to oven and roast for about 40 minutes or until golden in color.
- In the meantime, place ½ tablespoon olive oil in a pan and sauté mushrooms for about 4 minutes.
- Remove the cooked mushrooms from pan and set aside.
- Add the remaining olive oil to pan and sauté chopped spinach until tender.
- In a mixing bowl, combine together both types of ricotta and egg whites; set aside.
- Combine together all the vegetables, including grape tomatoes and peppers, with sourdough rolls in a 9 x 13

baking dish; top with the ricotta mixture and sprinkle with pecorino and mozzarella cheese.
- Bake for at least 40 minutes or until done. Remove from the oven, cool slightly.
- Cut into six slices and enjoy your breakfast.

# Egg and Sausage Breakfast Casserole

Total time: 1 hour, 25 minutes
Prep time: 20 minutes
Cook time: 1 hour, 5 minutes
Yield: 12 servings

## Ingredients
### The crust:
- 3 tbsp. olive oil, divided
- 2 lb. peeled and shredded russet potatoes
- ¾ tsp. ground pepper
- ¾ tsp. salt

### The casserole:
- 12 oz. chopped turkey sausage
- 4 thinly sliced green onions
- ¼ cup diced bell pepper
- ⅓ cup skim milk
- 6 large eggs
- 4 egg whites
- ¾ cup shredded cheddar cheese
- 16 oz. low-fat cottage cheese

## Directions
### The crust:
- Preheat the oven to 425°F. Lightly grease a 9×13-inch baking dish with 1 tbsp. olive oil and set aside.
- Squeeze excess moisture out of the potato with a kitchen towel or paper towel.
- Toss together the potatoes, the remaining olive oil, salt and pepper in a medium bowl until potatoes are well coated.
- Transfer the mixture to the greased baking dish; evenly press the mixture up the sides and on the bottom of the dish and bake for about 20 minutes or until golden brown on the edges.

### The casserole:
- Reduce the oven heat to 375°F.
- In a large skillet, cook turkey sausage over medium-high heat for about 2 minutes or until it's almost cooked through.

- Add green onions and red bell pepper and continue cooking for 2 more minutes or until bell pepper is tender.
- Whisk together skim milk, eggs, egg whites, and the cheeses.
- Stir in turkey sausage mixture; pour over the potato crust and bake for about 50 minutes. Slightly cool and cut into 12 pieces. Enjoy!

# Yogurt Pancakes

Total time: 15 minutes
Prep time: 10 minutes
Cooking time: 5 minutes
Yield: 5 servings

## Ingredients
- Whole-wheat pancake mix
- 1 cup yogurt
- 1 tbsp. baking powder
- 1 tbsp. baking soda
- 1 cup skimmed milk
- 3 whole eggs
- ½ tsp. extra virgin olive oil

## Directions
- Combine together whole-wheat pancake mix, yogurt, baking powder, baking soda, skimmed milk and eggs in large bowl.
- Stir until well blended.
- Heat a pan oiled lightly with olive oil.
- Pour ¼ cup batter onto the heated pan and cook for about 2 minutes or until the surface of the pancake has some bubbles.
- Flip and continue cooking until the underside is browned.
- Serve the pancakes warm with a cup of fat-free milk or two tablespoons light maple syrup.

# Breakfast Stir Fry

Total time:  25 minutes
Prep time: 5 minutes
Cooking time: 20 minutes
Yield:  4 servings

## Ingredients
- 1 tbsp. extra virgin olive oil
- 2 green peppers, sliced
- 2 small onions, finely chopped
- 4 tomatoes, chopped
- ½ tsp. sea salt
- 1 egg

## Directions
- Heat olive oil in a medium-sized pan over medium-high heat.
- Add green pepper and sauté for about 2 minutes.
- Lower heat to medium and continue cooking, covered, for 3 more minutes.
- Stir in onion and cook for about 2 minutes or until brown.
- Stir in tomatoes and salt; cover and simmer to get a soft juicy mixture.
- In a bowl, beat the egg; drizzle over the tomato mixture and cook for about 1 minute. (Don't stir).
- Serve with chopped cucumbers, feta cheese and black olives for a great breakfast!

# Greek Breakfast Pitas

Total time: 20 minutes
Prep time: 10 minutes
Cook time: 10 minutes
Yield: 4 servings

## Ingredients
- ¼ cup chopped onion
- ¼ cup sweet red/black pepper, chopped
- 1 cup large egg
- ⅛ tsp. sea salt
- ⅛ tsp. black pepper
- 1 ½ tsp. fresh basil, ground
- ½ cup baby spinach, freshly torn
- 1 red tomato, sliced
- 2 pita bread, whole
- 2 tbsp. feta cheese, crumbled

## Directions
- Coat a sizeable nonstick skillet with cooking spray and set over medium heat.
- Add onions and red peppers and sauté for at least 3 minutes.
- In a small bowl, beat together egg, pepper and salt and add the mixture to the skillet.
- Cook, stirring continuously, until ready.
- Spoon basil, spinach, and tomatoes onto the pitas and top with the egg mixture.
- Sprinkle with feta and serve.

# Healthy Breakfast Scramble

Total time: 20 minutes
Prep time: 5 minutes
Cook time: 15 minutes
Yield: 2 servings

## Ingredients
- 1 tsp. extra virgin olive
- 4 medium green onions, chopped
- 1 tsp. dried basil leaves or 1 tbsp. fresh basil leaves, chopped
- 1 medium tomato, chopped
- 4 eggs
- Freshly ground pepper

## Directions
- In a medium nonstick skillet, heat olive oil over medium heat; sauté green onions, stirring occasionally, for about 2 minutes.
- Stir in basil and tomato and let cook, stirring occasionally, for about 1 minute or until the tomato is cooked through.
- In a small bowl, thoroughly beat the eggs with a wire whisk or a fork and pour over the tomato mixture; cook for about 2 minutes.
- Gently lift the cooked parts with spatula to allow the uncooked parts to flow to the bottom.
- Continue cooking for about 3 minutes or until the eggs are cooked through.
- Season with pepper and serve.

# Greek Parfait

Total time: 6 minutes
Prep time: 6 minutes
Cook time: 0 minutes
Yield: 6 servings

## Ingredients
- 1 tsp. vanilla extract
- 3 cups low-fat Greek yogurt
- ¼ cup toasted unsalted pistachios, shelled
- 4 tsp. raw honey
- 28 Clementine segments

## Directions
- In a mixing bowl, combine the vanilla extract with the Greek yogurt.
- Spoon ¼ cup of the mixture into 4 small parfait glasses.
- Top each of the 4 glasses with ½ tablespoon nuts, ½ teaspoon honey and 5 Clementine sections.
- Add the remaining yogurt mixture to the parfait glasses and top with ½ tablespoon nuts, Clementine segments and ½ teaspoon honey.
- Serve immediately

# Quiche Wrapped in Prosciutto

Total time: 25 minutes
Prep time: 10 minutes
Cook time: 15 minutes
Yield: 8 servings

## Ingredients
- 4 slices prosciutto, halved
- 2 egg whites
- 1 egg
- ½ tsp. rosemary, fresh and chopped and a little more for garnishing
- 3tbsp. low fat Greek yoghurt
- 1 tbsp. chopped black olives
- A pinch of black pepper, freshly ground
- A pinch of salt

## Directions
- Preheat your oven to 400°F and coat your muffin baking tray with cooking spray.
- Place each prosciutto piece into eight cups of the tray.
- In a medium bowl, whisk the egg whites and the egg until smooth.
- Pour in the yogurt, rosemary, olives, pepper, and salt and continue whisking.
- Divide the mixture equally among the prosciutto cups and bake uncovered until cooked through (about 15 minutes).
- Garnish with rosemary.

# Morning Couscous

Total time: 35 minutes
Prep time 10 minutes
Cook time 25 minutes
Yield: 4 servings

## Ingredients
- 3 cups soy milk
- 1 cinnamon stick
- 1 cup whole-wheat couscous, uncooked
- ¼ cup currants, dried
- ½ cup apricots, dried
- 4 tsp. sun butter, melted and divided
- 6 tsp. brown sugar, divided
- 1 pinch salt

## Directions
- Put a saucepan on medium heat and pour in soy milk and the cinnamon stick.
- Let it heat for 3 minutes or until tiny bubbles start forming on the inner part of the pan; do not let it boil.
- Remove the saucepan from the heat and stir in the couscous, currants, apricots, salt, and 4 tablespoons of sugar.
- Put a lid on the pan and let it stand for 20 minutes. Remove the cinnamon stick.
- Divide the couscous among 4 bowls and top with ½ teaspoon of sugar and 1 teaspoon melted sun butter.
- Serve hot.

# Green Omelet

Total time: 15 minutes
Prep time: 5 minutes
Cook time: 10 minutes
Yield: 4 servings

## Ingredients
- 8 eggs
- 1 yellow onion, finely chopped
- 1 clove garlic, minced
- 1 medium bunch of collard greens
- 3 tbsp. parsley, chopped
- 1 tsp. allspice
- 5 tbsp. extra virgin olive oil
- ½ cup Parmigiano-Reggiano cheese, grated
- 1 pinch sea salt, optional

## Directions
- Beat the eggs in a big bowl and add the onion, garlic, collard greens, parsley, and allspice.
- Continue beating until all the ingredients mix well.
- Put a non-stick skillet on medium heat and pour in the olive oil until hot.
- Add the contents of the bowl and let cook for about 5 minutes or until it turns golden brown.
- Use a spatula to flip the omelet and cook the other side for 5 minutes or until it turns golden brown.
- Serve on a plate, cut into desired portions, then sprinkle the grated cheese and you are ready to eat.

# Healthy Quinoa

Total time: 25 minutes
Prep time: 10 minutes
Cook time: 15 minutes
Yield: 4 servings

## Ingredients
- 1 cup almonds
- 1 tsp. ground cinnamon
- 1 cup quinoa
- 2 cups milk
- 1 pinch sea salt
- 2 tbsp. honey
- 5 dried apricots, finely chopped
- 2 dried, pitted dates, finely chopped
- 1 tsp. vanilla extract

## Directions
- Start by toasting the almonds on a skillet for five minutes or until golden brown for a good nutty flavor.
- Place a saucepan over medium heat and add the quinoa and cinnamon; heat until warmed through.
- Follow by adding the milk and sea salt while stirring all along.
- Once the mixture comes to a boil, reduce the heat, cover the saucepan and let it simmer for 15 minutes.
- Add the honey, apricots, dates, vanilla extract and half the almonds into the saucepan.
- Serve in bowls and top with the remaining almonds.

# Energizing Breakfast Protein Bars

Total time: 45 minutes
Prep time: 10 minutes
Cook time: 35 minutes
Yield: 6 servings

## Ingredients
- ¼ cup pecans, chopped
- 2 tbsp. pistachios, chopped
- ¼ cup flaxseeds, ground
- 1 ¼ cup spelt flakes
- ½ cup dried cherries
- 1 pinch sea salt
- ½ cup honey
- 2 tbsp. extra virgin olive oil
- ¼ cup peanut butter, natural
- ½ tsp. vanilla extract

## Directions
- Start by preheating your oven to 325°F, then brush your baking tray with oil.
- Line the baking tray with parchment paper all round and brush it with oil.
- Combine the pecans, pistachios, flaxseeds, spelt, cherries, and salt in a mixing bowl and set aside.
- Place a saucepan over medium heat and pour in the honey, oil, peanut butter, and vanilla extract and cook, stirring, until the mixture melts.
- Add this mixture to the bowl of dry ingredients and mix well.
- Pour the mixture into the prepared baking tray and smooth the top.
- Bake until it turns golden brown and the sides pull out from the edges of the pan.
- Transfer the baked bar from the tray and cut it into smaller sizes on a cutting board.
- After cooling, store in an airtight container lined with parchment paper.
- The bars can last up to one week.

# Fruity Nutty Muesli

Total time: 1 hour 15 minutes
Prep time 15 minutes
Cook time 1 hour
Yield: 2 servings

## Ingredients
- ⅓ cup almonds, chopped
- ¾ cup oats, toasted
- ½ cup low-fat milk
- ½ cup low-fat Greek yogurt
- ½ green apple, diced
- 2 tbsp. raw honey

## Directions
- Preheat oven to 350°F. Place the almonds on a baking sheet and bake until they turn golden brown, about 10 minutes.
- After cooling, mix with the toasted oats, milk and yogurt in a bowl and cover.
- Refrigerate this mixture for an hour until the oats are soft.
- Divide the muesli between two bowls, add the apple and drizzle the honey.

# Egg Veggie Scramble

Total time: 30 minutes
Prep time 15 minutes
Cook time 15 minutes
Yield: 2 servings

## Ingredients
- 2 tsp. extra virgin olive oil, divided
- 1 medium orange bell pepper, diced
- ½ cup frozen corn kernels
- 1 scallion, thinly sliced
- ¼ tsp. cumin, freshly ground
- ¼ tsp. allspice, plus a pinch
- 2 eggs
- 2 egg whites
- Pinch of cinnamon
- ⅓ cup white cheddar, shredded
- 1 medium avocado, diced
- ½ cup fresh salsa
- 2 whole-wheat flour tortillas, warmed

## Directions
- Heat a teaspoon of olive oil in a non-stick pan over medium heat.
- Add bell pepper, tossing and turning for 5 minutes until soft; add the corn, scallion, cumin, and allspice and cook for a further 3 minutes until the scallion wilts.
- Pour this out onto a plate and cover it with foil. Wipe the pan clean with a paper towel and set it aside.
- Place the eggs and egg whites in a bowl and whisk them together with 2 teaspoons of water, a pinch of allspice and a pinch of cinnamon.
- Heat the remaining olive oil in the pan over medium heat and add the egg mixture.
- Cook until the bottom sets, about 30 seconds, then stir gently.
- Continue stirring for about 2 minutes, then add the shredded cheese and vegetables that you had wrapped in foil.
- Serve with avocado, salsa and the tortillas.

# Mediterranean Salad Recipes

## Grilled Tofu with Mediterranean Salad

Total time: 45 minutes
Prep time: 30 minutes
Cook time: 15 minutes
Yield: 4 servings

**Ingredients**
- 1 tbsp. extra virgin olive oil
- ¼ cup lemon juice
- 2 tsp. dried oregano
- 3 cloves garlic, minced
- ½ tsp. sea salt
- Freshly ground pepper
- 14 ounces water-packed extra-firm tofu

**Mediterranean Chopped Salad**
- 2 tbsp. extra virgin olive oil
- ¼ cup coarsely chopped Kalamata olives
- ¼ cup chopped scallions
- 1 cup diced seedless cucumber
- 2 medium tomatoes, diced
- ¼ cup chopped fresh parsley
- 1 tbsp. white-wine vinegar
- Freshly ground pepper
- ¼ tsp. sea salt

**Directions**
- Preheat your grill.
- In a small bowl, combine extra virgin olive oil, lemon juice, oregano, garlic, sea salt and black pepper; reserve two tablespoons of the mixture for basting.
- Drain tofu and rinse; pat dry with paper towels. Cut tofu crosswise into 8 ½-inch thick slices and put in a glass dish.
- Add the lemon juice marinade and turn tofu to coat well.
- Marinate in the fridge for at least 30 minutes.
- In the meantime, prepare the salad.
- In a medium bowl, combine all the salad ingredients; toss gently to mix well.

- Set aside.
- Brush the grill rack with oil. Drain the marinated tofu and discard the marinade.
- Grill tofu over medium heat, for about 4 minutes per side, basting frequently with the remaining lemon juice marinade.
- Serve grilled tofu warm, topped with the salad.

# Mediterranean Barley Salad

Total time: 1 hour 45 minutes
Prep time: 15 minutes
Cook time: 30 minutes
Chilling time: 1 hour
Yield: 6 servings

## Ingredients
- 2 ½ cups water
- 1 cup barley
- 4 tbsp. extra virgin olive oil, divided
- 2 cloves garlic
- 7 sun-dried tomatoes
- 1 tbsp. balsamic vinegar
- ½ cup chopped black olives
- ½ cup finely chopped cilantro

## Directions
- Mix water and barley in a saucepan; bring the mixture to a rolling boil over high heat.
- Lower heat to medium-low and simmer, covered, for about 30 minutes or until tender, but still a bit firm in the center.
- Drain and transfer to a large bowl; let the cooked barley cool to room temperature.
- In a blender, puree 2 tablespoons of extra virgin olive oil, garlic, sun-dried tomatoes, and balsamic vinegar until very smooth; pour over barley and fold in the remaining olive oil, olives, and cilantro.
- Refrigerate, covered, until chilled.
- Stir to mix well before serving.

# Mediterranean Quinoa Salad

Total time: 35 minutes
Prep time: 15 minutes
Cook time: 20 minutes
Yield: 4 servings

## Ingredients
- 1 clove garlic, smashed
- 2 cups water
- 2 cubes chicken bouillon
- 1 cup uncooked quinoa
- ½ cup chopped Kalamata olives
- 1 large red onion, diced
- 2 large chicken breasts (cooked), diced
- 1 large green bell pepper, diced
- ½ cup crumbled feta cheese
- ¼ cup chopped fresh chives
- ¼ cup chopped fresh parsley
- ½ tsp. sea salt
- ¼ cup extra virgin olive oil
- 1 tbsp. balsamic vinegar
- ⅔ cup fresh lemon juice

## Directions
- Combine garlic clove, water, and bouillon cubes in a saucepan; bring the mixture to a gentle boil over medium-low heat.
- Stir in quinoa and simmer, covered, for about 20 minutes or until the water has been absorbed and quinoa is tender.
- Discard garlic clove and transfer the cooked quinoa to a large bowl.
- Stir in olives, onion, chicken, bell pepper, feta cheese, chives, parsley, sea salt, extra virgin olive oil, balsamic vinegar, and lemon juice.
- Serve warm or chilled.

# Healthy Greek Salad

Total time: 15 minutes
Prep time: 15 minutes
Cook time: 0 minutes
Yield: 6 servings

## Ingredients
- 1 small red onion, chopped
- 2 cucumbers, peeled and chopped
- 3 large ripe tomatoes, chopped
- 4 tsp. freshly squeezed lemon juice
- ¼ cup extra virgin olive oil
- 1 ½ tsp. dried oregano
- Sea salt
- Ground black pepper
- 6 pitted and sliced black Greek olives
- 1 cup crumbled feta cheese

## Directions
- Combine onion, cucumber, and tomatoes in a shallow salad bowl; sprinkle with lemon juice, extra virgin olive, oregano, sea salt and black pepper.
- Sprinkle the olives and feta over the salad and serve immediately.

# Almond, Mint and Kashi Salad

Total time: 1 hour 35 minutes
Prep time: 15 minutes
Cook time: 1 hour
Cooling time: 20 minutes
Yield: 4 servings

## Ingredients
- 4 tbsp. extra virgin olive oil, divided, plus more for drizzling
- 1 small onion, finely chopped
- Sea salt, to taste
- Freshly ground black pepper, to taste
- 2 cups water
- 1 cup Kashi 7-Whole Grain Pilaf
- 2 bay leaves
- 3 tbsp. fresh lemon juice
- 5 tbsp. sliced natural almonds, divided
- 8 cherry tomatoes, quartered
- ¼ cup chopped parsley
- ¼ cup chopped fresh mint
- 4 large romaine leaves

## Directions
- Heat 2 tablespoons of extra virgin olive oil in a large saucepan set over medium heat.
- Add onion, sea salt and pepper and cook, stirring occasionally, for about 5 minutes or until lightly browned and tender.
- Stir in 2 cups of water, Kashi, bay leaves, sea salt and pepper; bring the mixture to a rolling boil, lower heat to a simmer and cook, covered, for about 40 minutes or until Kashi is tender.
- Transfer to a large bowl and discard bay leaves, and then stir in the remaining extra virgin olive oil, and lemon juice.
- Let sit for at least 20 minutes or until cooled to room temperature.
- Adjust the seasoning if desired and add 4 tablespoons almonds, tomatoes, parsley, and mint; toss to mix well.

- Place one romaine leaf on each of the four plates and spoon the mixture into the center of the leaves; drizzle with extra virgin olive oil and sprinkle with the remaining almonds.

# Chickpea Salad

Total time: 1 hour, 20 minutes
Prep time: 10 minutes
Cook time: 40 minutes
Standing time: 30 minutes
Yield: 6 servings

## Ingredients
- 1 ½ cups dried chickpeas, soaked and liquid reserved
- 1 ¼ tsp. sea salt, divided
- 1 garlic clove, minced
- 2 tbsp. extra virgin olive oil
- 3 tbsp. sherry vinegar
- 16 crushed whole black peppercorns
- ¾ tsp. dried oregano
- 3 scallions, sliced into ½-inch pieces
- 2 carrots (4 ounces), cut into ½-inch dice
- 1 cup diced green bell pepper
- ½ English cucumber, peeled and diced
- 2 cups halved cherry tomatoes
- 2 tbsp. shredded fresh basil
- 3 tbsp. chopped fresh parsley

## Directions
- Combine the chickpeas and soaking liquid in a large pot and season with ¾ teaspoons of sea salt.
- Bring the mixture to a gentle boil over medium heat. Lower heat to a simmer and cook, stirring occasionally, for about 40 minutes or until the chickpeas are tender; drain and transfer to a large bowl.
- In the meantime, mash together garlic and salt to form a paste; transfer to a separate bowl and stir in extra virgin olive oil, vinegar, peppercorns, and oregano to make the dressing.
- Pour the garlic dressing over the chickpeas and let stand for at least 30 minutes, stirring once.
- Toss in scallions, carrots, bell pepper, cucumber, tomatoes, basil, and parsley.
- Serve.

# Italian Bread Salad

Total time: 2 hours 30 minutes
Prep time: 25 minutes, plus 2 hours Refrigerator time
Cook time: 5 minutes
Yield: 4 servings

## Ingredients
- 3 tbsp. freshly squeezed lemon juice
- 2 tbsp. extra virgin olive oil
- Sea salt
- Freshly ground pepper
- 1 red onion, halved and sliced
- 1 bulb fennel, stalks removed and sliced
- 1 peeled English cucumber, sliced
- 1 ½ pounds diced tomatoes
- ⅓ cup pitted Kalamata olives, halved
- 4 slices whole-wheat country bread
- 1 garlic clove, peeled and halved
- 4 ounces shaved ricotta salata cheese
- ½ cup fresh basil leaves

## Directions
- Whisk together lemon juice and extra virgin olive oil in a large bowl; season with sea salt and black pepper.
- Stir in onion, fennel, cucumber, tomatoes, and olives; toss to combine and refrigerate for about 2 hours.
- When ready, heat your broiler with the rack positioned 4 inches from heat and toast the bread on a baking sheet for about 2 minutes per side or until lightly browned.
- Transfer the toasted bread to a work surface and rub with the cut garlic and cut it into 2-inch pieces.
- Divide the bread among four shallow bowls and top with the tomato salad; sprinkle with cheese and basil to serve.

# Bulgur Salad

Total time: 30 minutes
Prep time: 10 minutes
Cook time: 20 minutes
Yield: 4 servings

## Ingredients
- 1 tbsp. unsalted butter
- 2 tbsp. extra virgin olive oil, divided
- 2 cups bulgur
- 4 cups water
- ¼ tsp. sea salt
- 1 medium cucumber, deseeded and chopped
- ¼ cup dill, chopped
- 1 handful black olives, pitted and chopped
- 2 tsp. red wine vinegar

## Directions
- Place a saucepan over medium heat and add 1 tbsp. of butter and 1 tbsp. of olive oil.
- Toast the bulgur in the oil until it turns golden brown and starts to crackle.
- Add 4 cups of water to the saucepan and season with the salt.
- Cover the saucepan and simmer until all the water gets absorbed for about 20 minutes.
- In a mixing bowl, combine the chopped cucumber with dill, olives, red wine vinegar and the remaining olive oil.
- Serve this over the bulgur.

# Greek Salad

Total time: 20 minutes
Prep time: 20 minutes
Cook time: 0 minutes
Yield: 4 servings

## Ingredients
- Juice of 1 lemon
- 6 tbsp. extra virgin olive oil
- Black pepper to taste, ground
- 1 tsp. oregano, dried
- 1 head romaine lettuce, washed, dried and chopped
- 1 red bell pepper, chopped
- 1 green bell pepper, chopped
- 1 cucumber, sliced
- 2 tomatoes, chopped
- 1 cup feta cheese, crumbled
- 1 red onion, thinly sliced
- 1 can black olives, pitted

## Directions
- Whisk together the lemon juice, olive oil, pepper and oregano in a small bowl.
- In a large bowl, combine the lettuce, bell peppers, cucumber, tomatoes, cheese and onion.
- Pour the salad dressing into this bowl and toss until evenly coated with the dressing, then serve.

# Potato Salad

Total time: 24 minutes
Prep time: 10 minutes
Cook time: 14 minutes
Yield: 4 servings

## Ingredients
- 5 medium potatoes, peeled and diced
- Coarse salt, to taste
- ¼ onion
- 3 tbsp. yellow mustard
- 2 cups mayonnaise
- 1 tsp. paprika, sweet
- 1 tsp. Tabasco
- 2 scallions, thinly sliced

## Directions
- Pour some water in a saucepan and place over medium heat.
- Add the potatoes, season with coarse salt and boil for around 10 minutes until tender.
- Drain the water and return the saucepan to the heat to dry them out.
- Let the potatoes cool to room temperature.
- Grate the onion in a mixing bowl, add mustard, mayo, paprika and the hot sauce and mix well.
- Add the potatoes to the bowl and toss until evenly coated.
- Divide among four bowls and top with the sliced scallions.

# Mediterranean Green Salad

Total time: 25 minutes
Prep time: 15 minutes
Cook time: 10 minutes
Yield: 4 servings

## Ingredients
- ½ loaf rustic sourdough bread
- ¼ tsp. paprika
- 2 tbsp. manchego, finely grated
- 7 tbsp. extra virgin olive oil, divided
- 1 ½ tbsp. sherry vinegar
- ½ tsp. sea salt
- 1 tsp. freshly ground black pepper
- 1 tsp. Dijon mustard
- 5 cups mixed baby greens
- ¾ cup green olives, pitted and halved
- 12 thin slices of Serrano ham, roughly chopped

## Directions
- Cut the bread into bite-sized cubes and set aside.
- Preheat oven to 400°F.
- In a mixing bowl, combine paprika, manchego and 6 tbsps. of olive oil.
- Add the bread cubes and toss them until they are evenly coated with the flavored oil.
- Arrange the bread on a baking sheet and bake for about 8 minutes until golden brown and let the bread cool.
- In a separate bowl, combine the vinegar, salt, pepper, mustard and the remaining olive oil.
- Add this mixture to a larger bowl containing the greens until they are lightly coated with the vinaigrette.
- Add all the other ingredients and the croutons and toss well.
- Serve the salad on four plates.
- This salad has an amazing taste and leaves you energized to face the remaining part of the day.

# Chickpea Salad with Yogurt Dressing

Total time: 30 minutes
Prep time: 30 minutes
Cook time: 0 minutes
Yield: 4 servings

## Ingredients
### Dressing
- 1 tbsp. freshly squeezed lemon juice
- 1 cup plain nonfat Greek yogurt
- ¼ tsp. cayenne pepper
- 1½ tsp. curry powder

### Salad
- 2 15-oz. cans chickpeas, rinsed and drained
- 1 cup diced red apple
- ½ cup diced celery
- ¼ cup chopped walnuts
- ¼ cup thinly sliced green onions
- ⅓ cup raisins
- ½ cup chopped fresh parsley
- 2 lemon wedges

## Directions
**Make dressing:** In a small bowl, whisk together lemon juice, yogurt, cayenne, and curry powder until well combined.
**Make salad:** In a large bowl, toss together chickpeas, apple, celery, walnuts, green onions, raisins, and parsley.
Gently fold in the dressing and season with sea salt and pepper.
Serve garnished with lemon wedges.

# Warm Lentil Salad

Total time: 20 minutes
Prep time: 10 minutes
Cook time: 10 minutes
Yield: 4 servings

## Ingredients
- 3 tbsp. extra virgin olive oil
- 1 ½ cups thinly sliced leeks
- 2 tsp. whole-grain mustard
- 2 tbsp. sherry vinegar
- 2 cups cooked lentils
- 1 ½ cups red grapes, halved
- ¼ cup chopped roasted pistachios
- ¼ cup crumbled feta
- 3 tbsp. finely chopped parsley
- 3 tbsp. finely chopped mint

## Directions
- In a skillet, heat extra virgin olive oil over medium heat; add leeks and sauté, stirring, for about 9 minutes or until translucent and tender.
- Remove the pan from heat and stir in mustard and sherry vinegar.
- In a large bowl, combine the leek mixture, lentils, grapes, pistachios, mint, parsley, sea salt, and pepper.
- Top with feta and enjoy!

# Mediterranean Soup and Stew Recipes

## Leeky Parsley Soup

Total time: 35 minutes
Prep time: 20 minutes
Cook time: 15 minutes
Yields: 4 to 6 servings

## Ingredients

- 1 tbsp. olive oil
- 1 bunch fresh flat-leaf parsley, stems chopped, parsley leaves reserved for garnishing
- 2 large or 3 medium leeks, pale green and white parts chopped
- 4 cups of water
- 4 cups low-sodium vegetable or chicken broth or 4 cups of water
- 4 green onions (about 3-inch green parts and white parts), chopped
- 1 medium unpeeled zucchini, shredded with a grater
- 2 tsp. salt

## Directions

- Add oil to a large stockpot set over medium high heat.
- Add parsley and the leeks to the oil and cook, stirring continuously for about 5 minutes or until leeks become light in color.
- Add broth or water, green onions and zucchini and bring the mixture to a boil.
- Lower heat to medium and simmer for about 10 minutes.
- Remove from heat and cool the soup for about 10 minutes.
- Serve warm, garnished with parsley leaves.

# Tasty Lentil Soup

Total time: 1 hour 20 minutes
Prep time: 20 minutes
Cook time: 1 hour
Yield: 4 servings

## Ingredients
- 1 ½ cups brown lentils
- ¼ cup olive oil
- 1 large onion, chopped
- 2 cloves garlic, pressed
- 1 carrot, chopped
- ¼ tsp. dried oregano
- ¼ tsp. dried rosemary
- 2 bay leaves, dried
- 1 tbsp. tomato paste
- 1 tsp. red wine vinegar

## Directions
- Pour the lentils in a large saucepan and cover with water.
- Place over medium heat and bring to a boil; cook for 10 – 20 minutes and drain in a strainer.
- Clean the saucepan and pour in the olive oil and bring to medium heat.
- Add the onions and garlic and cook until the onions are soft, then add the carrots and cook for a further 5 minutes.
- Pour in the lentils and 1 ½ cups of water, oregano, rosemary and bay leaves.
- Once the pan comes to a boil, reduce the heat and simmer for 10 minutes.
- Add the tomato paste and continue simmering until the lentils soften for about 30 minutes stirring.
- Add water to get the consistency of soup you like.
- Drizzle with the vinegar to taste.

# Veggie Barley Soup

Total time: 1 hour 45 minutes
Prep time: 15 minutes
Cook time: 1 hour 30 minutes
Yield: 4 servings

## Ingredients

- 2 quarts vegetable broth
- 2 stalks celery, chopped
- 2 large carrots, chopped
- 1 cup barley
- 1 (15 ounce) can garbanzo beans, drained
- 1 zucchini, chopped
- 1 (14.5 ounce) can tomatoes with juice
- 1 onion, chopped
- 3 bay leaves
- 1 tsp. dried parsley
- 1 tsp. white sugar
- 1 tsp. garlic powder
- 1 tsp. Worcestershire sauce
- 1 tsp. paprika
- 1 tsp. curry powder
- ½ tsp. ground black pepper
- 1 tsp. sea salt

## Directions

- Add broth to a large soup pot over medium heat.
- Stir in celery, carrots, barley, garbanzo beans, zucchini, tomatoes, onion, bay leaves, parsley, sugar, garlic powder, Worcestershire sauce, paprika, curry powder, sea salt and pepper.
- Bring the mixture to a gentle boil; cover and lower heat to medium low.
- Cook for about 90 minutes or until the soup is thick.
- Discard bay leaves and serve hot.

# Chickpea Soup

Total time: 50 minutes
Prep time: 20 minutes
Cook time: 30 minutes
Yield: 6 servings

## Ingredients
- 1 tbsp. extra virgin olive oil
- 4 cloves garlic, minced
- 1 cup diced onion
- 2 (15-oz.) cans chickpeas, rinsed, drained
- ¼ cup freshly squeezed lemon juice
- ½ cup chopped parsley
- 1 bay leaf
- 1 ½ tsp. sea salt
- Moroccan Spice Oil

## Directions
- Heat extra virgin olive oil in a medium saucepan set over medium heat; add garlic and onion and sauté, stirring, for about 10 minutes or until starts to brown.
- Add 4 cups of water, chickpeas, parsley and bay leaf; stir and bring to a gentle boil, covered.
- Reduce heat and simmer for about 15 minutes.
- Stir in sea salt and discard bay leaf.
- In batches, puree the soup in a food processor until very smooth and creamy.
- Return the pureed soup back to the pan and stir in lemon juice.
- Ladle the soup into bowls and drizzle with about ½ teaspoon Moroccan Spice Oil and sprinkle with parsley.
- Enjoy!

# Red Lentil Bean Soup

Total time: 1 hour
Prep time: 15 minutes
Cook time: 45 minutes
Yield: 4 servings

## Ingredients

- 2 cups dried red lentil beans, rinsed
- 2 tbsp. extra virgin olive oil, plus more for drizzling
- 2 large onions, diced
- 1 - 2 finely chopped carrots
- 8 cups chicken stock
- 2 ripe tomatoes, cubed
- 1 tsp. ground cumin
- Sea salt
- Black pepper
- 2 cups fresh spinach

## Directions

- Soak lentils for at least 2 hours.
- In a pot set over medium high heat, boil the lentils until almost cooked.
- In a soup pot, heat extra virgin olive oil over medium heat; add diced onions and carrots and sauté for about 4 minutes or until tender.
- Add stock, tomatoes, cumin, sea salt and pepper and simmer for about 40 minutes or until lentils are tender.
- Stir in spinach until just wilted and drizzle with extra virgin olive oil just before serving.

# Chickpea and Lentil Bean Soup

Total time: 1 hour 15 minutes
Prep time: 15 minutes
Cook time: 1 hour
Yield: 4 servings

## Ingredients
- 2 tbsp. extra virgin olive oil
- 2 large onions, diced
- 2 cloves garlic, minced
- 4 large celery stalks, diced
- 1 cup dried lentils, rinsed
- 6 cups water
- ½ tsp. grated fresh ginger
- ½ tsp. cinnamon
- ¾ tsp. turmeric
- 1 tsp. cumin
- sea salt to taste
- 1 (16-ounce) can chickpeas, rinsed
- 3 ripe tomatoes, cubed
- Juice of ½ lemon
- ½ cup chopped cilantro or parsley
- ½ lemon, thinly sliced

## Directions
- In a soup pot, heat extra virgin olive oil; add onions and sauté for about 5 minutes or until fragrant and tender.
- Stir in garlic and celery and sauté for 3 minutes more or until onions are golden.
- Stir in lentils, 6 cups of water and spices and bring the mixture to a gentle boil over medium high heat; lower heat to medium-low and simmer for about 40 minutes or until the lentils are tender.
- Stir in chickpeas, tomatoes, and more water and spices, if needed.
- Simmer for about 15 minutes more.
- Stir in freshly squeezed lemon juice, cilantro or parsley and ladle the soup into serving bowl.
- Garnish each serving with 1 or 2 lemon slices and serve immediately.

# Fish Soup with Rotelle

Total time: 45 minutes
Prep time: 15 minutes
Cook time: 30 minutes
Yield: 4 servings

## Ingredients
- 2 tbsp. extra virgin olive oil, plus more for drizzling
- 1 tbsp. minced garlic
- 1 onion, diced
- ½ can crushed tomatoes
- 1 cup rotelle pasta
- ¼ tsp. rosemary
- 1 dozen mussels in their shells
- 1 pound monkfish

## Directions
- In a saucepan over medium heat, heat extra virgin olive oil; add garlic and onion and sauté for about 4 minutes or until soft.
- Stir in tomatoes, water, pasta, and rosemary; season with sea salt and pepper and cook for about 15 minutes.
- Clean mussels and cut monkfish into small pieces; stir into the soup and simmer for about 10 minutes more, or until all mussel shells open.
- Discard unopened shells and serve soup drizzled with more extra virgin olive oil, with crusty bread.

# Bean and Cabbage Soup

Total time: 1 hour
Prep time: 10 minutes
Cook time: 50 minutes
Yield: 6 servings

## Ingredients
- ¼ cup olive oil
- ½ cup chopped onion
- 2 celery stalks, chopped
- 2 carrots, chopped
- One 14.5-ounce can diced tomatoes
- ¼ tsp. dried sage
- 6 sprigs parsley
- 1 bay leaf
- 8 cups water
- 1 (14.5-ounce) can cannellini beans, drained
- ½ pound baked ham, diced
- 6 cups chopped green cabbage
- ½ pound Yukon potatoes, diced
- ¼ cup instant polenta
- Sea salt
- Black pepper

## Directions
- In a large stock pot set over medium heat, heat extra virgin olive oil until hot; stir in onions, celery and carrots and sauté for about 7 minutes or until onions are translucent.
- Stir in tomatoes, sage, parsley, and bay leaf; lower heat to low and simmer for about 10 minutes.
- Stir in water and bring to a rolling boil over medium high heat.
- Stir in beans, ham, cabbage, and potatoes and reduce heat to medium-low.
- Cook for about 20 minutes or until potatoes are tender.
- Stir in polenta; simmer for about 5 minutes and season with sea salt and pepper.
- Ladle the soup into bowls and serve immediately.

# Minestrone Soup

Total time: 8 hours 15 minutes
Prep time: 15 minutes
Cook time: 8 hours
Yield: 8 servings

## Ingredients
- 1 onion, diced
- 1 (28-ounce) can diced tomatoes
- 2 (14.5-ounce) cans navy beans, rinsed
- 3 celery stalks, sliced
- 3 carrots, washed, sliced
- 4 Italian chicken sausage links, sliced
- 4 cups chicken stock
- 3 zucchinis, sliced
- 1 cup orzo
- Sea salt
- ½ cup grated Parmesan
- 1/2 tsp. dried sage
- 2 bay leaves
- 2 sprigs thyme
- Sea salt

## Directions
- In a 5-quart slow cooker over low heat, stir together onions, tomatoes, beans, celery, carrots, sausage, stock, sage, thyme, and bay leaves; cook for about 8 hours.
- Stir in zucchini and orzo during the last 30 minutes or cooking.
- Season with sea salt and divide the soup among 8 bowls, discard bay leaves and top each serving with a tablespoon of grated Parmesan cheese.
- Enjoy!

# Spicy Lentil and Spinach Soup

Total time: 35 minutes
Prep time: 5 minutes
Cook time: 30 minutes
Yield: 4 to 6 servings

## Ingredients

- 2 tbsp. extra virgin olive oil
- 1 large yellow onion, finely chopped
- 1 large garlic clove, chopped
- 2 tsp. dried mint flakes
- 1½ tsp. crushed red peppers
- 1½ tsp. sumac
- 1½ tsp. cumin
- 1½ tsp. coriander
- Sea salt
- Black pepper
- Pinch of sugar
- 1 tbsp. flour
- 3 cups water, more if needed
- 6 cups low-sodium vegetable broth
- 1½ cups small brown lentils, rinsed
- 10-12 oz. frozen cut leaf spinach (no need to thaw)
- 2 cups chopped parsley
- 2 tbsp. lime juice

## Directions

- Heat 2 tablespoons of extra virgin olive oil in a large ceramic pot over medium heat.
- Stir in chopped onions and sauté for about 4 minutes or until golden brown.
- Add garlic, dried mint, all spices, sugar and flour and cook for about 2 minutes, stirring frequently.
- Stir in water and broth and bring to a rolling mixture over medium high heat; stir in lentils and spinach and cook for about 5 minutes.

- Lower heat to medium low and cook, covered, for about 20 minutes or until lentils are tender.
- Stir in chopped parsley and lime juice and remove the pot from heat; set stand for at least 5 minutes for flavors to meld and serve hot with favorite rustic Italian bread or pita bread.

# Three-Bean Soup with Tomato Pesto

Total time: 50 minutes
Prep time: 20 minutes
Cook time: 30 minutes
Yield: 6 servings

## Ingredients
## Tomato Pesto Sauce
- 4-6 garlic cloves
- 1 cup diced tomatoes
- 15 large basil leaves
- ½ cup extra virgin olive oil
- ½ cup grated Parmesan cheese
- Sea salt
- Black pepper

## Soup ingredients
- 2 tbsp. extra virgin olive oil, plus more for drizzling
- 1 russet potato, peeled and diced
- 1½ cups diced tomatoes
- 8-oz French green beans, chopped
- 1 tsp. hot paprika
- 1 tbsp. coriander
- Sea salt
- Black pepper
- 1 tbsp. white vinegar
- 6 cups vegetable broth
- 2 cups cooked red kidney beans
- 2 cups cooked white kidney beans
- ⅓ cup toasted pine nuts
- Basil leaves
- Grated Parmesan

## Directions
Make tomato pesto sauce:
- Pulse together garlic and tomatoes in a food processor until well combined.
- Add basil and continue pulsing.
- Gradually add extra virgin olive oil and pulse until smooth.
- Transfer the pesto to a bowl and stir in grated Parmesan cheese; season to taste with salt and pepper and set aside.

- In a heavy pot or Dutch oven, heat 2 tablespoons extra virgin olive oil over medium high heat until hot but not smoky.
- Add diced potato and lower heat to medium.
- Cook, stirring occasionally, for about 4 minutes.
- Stir in tomatoes, green beans, spices and vinegar and stir to combine well; cook, covered, for about 4 minutes more.
- Remove the lid and raise heat to medium high; stir in vegetable broth and cook for about 5 minutes.
- Lower heat again to medium and cover the pot.
- Cook for about 10 minutes, and then stir in red and white kidney beans.
- Continue cooking for about 5 minutes or until the beans are heated through.
- Add tomato pesto and remove the pot from heat.
- Ladle the soup into bowls and drizzle each serving with extra virgin olive oil, toasted pine nuts, fresh basil leaves and grated Parmesan cheese.
- Serve with favorite Italian bread.

# Lemony Soup

Total time: 28 minutes
Prep time: 5 minutes
Cook time: 23 minutes
Yield: 8 servings

## Ingredients
- 8 cups low-sodium vegetable or chicken stock
- 2 tbsp. extra virgin olive oil
- ¼ cup flour
- 2 tbsp. butter
- 1 cup orzo
- 4 eggs
- ¾ cup freshly squeezed lemon juice
- Sea salt to taste
- ¼ tsp. ground white pepper
- 8 lemon slices

## Directions
- In a soup pot, bring stock to a gentle boil over medium heat; reduce heat to a simmer.
- In a small bowl, mix together extra virgin olive oil, flour and butter.
- Whisk 2 cups of hot stock into the flour mixture until well blended.
- Gradually beat the flour mixture into the pot with stock and simmer for about 10 minutes.
- Stir in orzo and continue cooking for about 5 minutes.
- In the meantime, beat the eggs and lemon juice in a small bowl until well blended and foamy.
- Slowly whisk a cup of hot soup mixture into the egg mixture until well combined.
- Add the egg mixture to the pot with the soup and stir to mix well.
- Simmer for about 10 minutes or until the soup is thick.
- Season with sea salt and pepper and ladle the soup into serving bowl.
- Serve right away garnished with lemon slices.

# Mediterranean Beef Stew with Red Wine

Total time: 28 minutes
Prep time: 5 minutes
Cook time: 23 minutes
Yield: 8 servings

## Ingredients
- 1 tbsp. extra virgin olive oil
- 1 onion, chopped
- ½ cup flour
- ½ tsp. sea salt
- 1 tsp. freshly ground black pepper
- 2 pounds beef shoulder chunks, cut into small pieces
- 2 cloves garlic
- 2 cups crimini mushrooms, halved
- 2 medium carrots, sliced
- 2 celery stalks, chopped
- 1 cup chopped parsley
- 1 14-ounce can diced tomatoes
- 1 tsp. dried oregano
- 1 tsp. granulated sugar
- 2 cups low-sodium beef stock
- 2 sprigs thyme
- 1 bay leaf
- 2 cups red wine

## Directions
- Heat extra virgin olive oil in a Dutch oven over medium high heat until hot but not smoky.
- Stir in onions and sauté for about 5 minutes or until lightly browned.
- Transfer the sautéed onions to a plate and set aside.
- In the meantime, combine flour, sea salt and black pepper in a large bowl; dredge meat in the flour mixture.
- Shake off excess flour and add the meat to the pan; cook for about 5 minutes per side or until browned on both sides.
- Return onions to the pan along with garlic, mushrooms, carrots, celery, oregano, thyme, and bay leaf.
- Stir in stock, tomatoes, wine, and sugar until well blended.
- Bring the mixture to a gentle boil and reduce heat to low.

- Cook for about 3 hours or until meat is tender.
- Stir in chopped parsley before serving.
- Serve over mashed potatoes, polenta, or orzo for a great meal.

# Chicken Stew with Plum Tomatoes and Chickpeas

Total time: 1 hour 27 minutes
Prep time: 12 minutes
Cook time: 1 hour 15 minutes
Yield: 6 servings

## Ingredients
- 2 tbsp. extra virgin olive oil
- 4 skinless chicken thighs
- 1 14-ounce can chickpeas, drained
- 1 celery stalk, chopped
- 1 tsp. turmeric
- ¼ tsp. ginger
- ½ tsp. cinnamon
- ¼ tsp. sea salt
- 1 tsp. freshly ground black pepper
- 1 28-ounce can plum tomatoes
- ½ cup long-grain rice
- ¼ cup red lentils
- 6 cups low-sodium chicken stock
- ¼ cup freshly squeezed lemon juice
- 1 onion, chopped
- ½ cup chopped cilantro

## Directions
- Heat extra virgin olive oil in a stockpot over medium high heat.
- Add chicken and cook for about 3 minutes per side or until lightly browned.
- Stir in onion, chickpeas, celery and spices and cook for about 3 minutes or until spices are heated through.
- Stir tomatoes, rice, lentils, and stock and bring the mixture to a gentle boil.
- Lower heat to low and simmer, covered, for about 15 minutes or until or until lentils are tender and stir in lemon juice.
- Divide the stew among six bowls and garnish each serving with 2 tablespoons of chopped cilantro to serve.

# Italian Potato and Leek Soup

Total time: 51 minutes
Prep time: 8 minutes
Cook time: 43 minutes
Yield: 6 servings

## Ingredients
- 2 tbsp. extra virgin olive oil
- 1 tbsp. butter
- 1 medium sweet onion, chopped
- 1 ½ pounds leeks (about 3 large stalks), rinsed and thinly sliced
- 1 cup dry white wine
- 3 pounds potatoes, peeled and diced
- 6 cups low-sodium chicken stock
- ½ cup whipping cream
- Sea salt to taste
- White pepper to taste

## Directions
- Heat extra virgin olive oil and butter in a large stockpot over medium high heat until butter is melted and foamy.
- Stir in onions and leeks and sauté for about 10 minutes or until tender and lightly browned. Stir in wine and cook for about 5 minutes.
- Stir in potatoes and stock and simmer for about 25 minutes or until potatoes are cooked through.
- Transfer the mixture to a blender and process until smooth and creamy.
- Return the soup to the pot and add the cream; simmer for about 3 minutes and season with sea salt and pepper.
- Serve immediately.

# Healthy Chicken Soup

Total time: 1 hour 5 minutes
Prep time: 25 minutes
Cook time: 40 minutes
Yield: 8 servings

## Ingredients
- 1 ½ pounds skinless, boneless chicken breasts, diced
- 1 tsp. black pepper
- 1 tbsp. Greek seasoning
- 1 tbsp. extra virgin olive oil
- 1 garlic clove, minced
- 4 green onions, thinly sliced
- ¼ cup white wine
- 7 cups low-sodium chicken broth
- 1 tbsp. capers, drained
- ¼ cup Greek olives, pitted, sliced
- ¼ cup chopped sun-dried tomatoes
- 1 ½ cups orzo pasta
- 1-1/2 tsp. minced fresh oregano
- 1-1/2 tsp. minced fresh basil
- 1 ½ tsp. minced fresh parsley
- 2 tbsp. fresh lemon juice

## Directions
- Generously season chicken with pepper and Greek seasoning.
- In a Dutch oven, heat extra virgin olive oil over medium high heat until hot but not smoky.
- Add chicken and sauté for about 10 minutes or until no longer pink; transfer to a plate and set aside.
- Add garlic and green onion to the pot and sauté for about 1 minute or until fragrant; stir in wine to loosen the browned bits; stir in chicken, broth, capers, olives, tomatoes, oregano and basil and bring the mixture to a boil.
- Lower heat and simmer, covered, for about 15 minutes.
- Raise heat and bring the mixture to a boil; stir in orzo and cook for about 10 minutes more or until pasta is tender.
- Stir in parsley and lemon juice and serve immediately.

# Tuscan Veggie Soup

Total time: 35 minutes
Prep time: 20 minutes
Cook time: 15 minutes
Yield: 6 servings

## Ingredients
- 1 (15-ounce) can cannellini beans, rinsed and divided
- 1 tbsp. extra virgin olive oil
- 1 cup diced onion
- 1 clove garlic, minced
- ½ cup diced celery
- ½ cup diced carrot
- 1 ½ cups diced zucchini
- 2 tsp. chopped sage leaves
- 1 tbsp. chopped thyme leaves
- ½ tsp. sea salt
- ¼ tsp. black pepper
- 1 (14.5-ounce) can diced tomatoes
- 32 ounces low-sodium chicken broth
- 2 cups chopped baby spinach
- ⅓ cup grated Parmesan

## Directions
- Mash half of beans in a small bowl and set aside.
- In a large soup pot, heat extra virgin olive oil over medium high heat; add onion, garlic, celery, carrots, zucchini, sage, thyme, sea salt and pepper.
- Cook, stirring occasionally, for about 5 minutes or until the vegetables are tender.
- Stir in tomatoes and broth and bring to a boil.
- Stir in the mashed, whole beans, and spinach, and cook for about 3 minutes more or until spinach is wilted.
- Ladle the soup into bowls, top with Parmesan cheese, and serve immediately.

# Roasted Veggie Soup

Total time: 1 hour 5 minutes
Prep time: 25 minutes
Cook time: 40 minutes
Yield: 4 servings

## Ingredients
- 5 garlic cloves
- 1 tbsp. extra virgin olive oil
- 2 green and yellow bell peppers, diced
- 350 g potatoes, diced
- ½ tsp. chopped rosemary
- 1 large red onion, diced
- 1 yellow zucchini, diced
- 1 ½ cups carrot juice
- 370 g Italian tomatoes, diced
- ½ tsp. chopped rosemary
- 1 tsp. fresh tarragon

## Directions
- Preheat your oven to 450ºF.
- In a roasting pan, combine garlic and extra virgin olive oil; roast in the preheated oven for about 5 minutes or until oil starts to sizzle.
- Add peppers, potatoes, and rosemary and toss to coat; continue roasting for about 15 minutes more or until potatoes are tender and golden.
- Add onion and yellow zucchini and roast for about 15 minutes more or until zucchini is tender.
- In a saucepan set over medium heat, combine tomatoes, carrot juice, and tarragon; bring to a boil.
- Add the roasted vegetables to the pan; add a small amount of water to the roasting pan and stir, scraping up browned bits that cling to the pan, and add to the saucepan.
- Cook for about 2 minutes or until heated through.
- Serve immediately.

# Moroccan Beef Stew

Total time: 30 minutes
Prep time: 10 minutes
Cook time: 20 minutes
Yield: 6 servings

## Ingredients
- 3 tbsp. extra virgin olive oil, divided
- 1 ¾ pounds beef tenderloin, diced
- Sea salt and pepper, to taste
- 2 garlic cloves, chopped
- 1 large carrot, chopped
- 1 large onion, chopped
- 1 ½ tsp. ground cinnamon
- 2 tsp. ground cumin
- 1 tbsp. paprika
- 1 15-ounce can garbanzo beans, drained
- ½ cup golden raisins
- ½ cup pitted Kalamata olives, diced
- 2 cups beef broth
- ½ cup chopped fresh cilantro
- 1 tsp. lemon zest

## Directions
- In a heavy large saucepan over medium high heat, heat 2 tablespoons extra virgin olive oil.
- Season beef with sea salt and pepper.
- Add beef to the pan and cook for about 3 minutes or until browned on all sides.
- Transfer to a plate and set aside.
- Add the remaining oil, garlic, carrot and onion to the pan and cook, stirring, for about 10 minutes or until the vegetables are tender.
- Stir in spices for about 1 minutes and add garbanzo beans, raisins, olives, broth, and cilantro; bring to a gentle boil.
- Reduce heat and simmer for about 5 minutes or until juices thicken.
- Add beef along with any accumulated juices.
- Stir in lemon zest and serve.

# Tuscan Bean Stew

Total time: 2 hours 30 minutes
Prep time: 30 minutes
Cook time: 2 hours
Yield: 6 servings

## Ingredients
- 3 tbsp. extra virgin olive oil, divided
- 2 cloves garlic, quartered
- 1 slice whole-grain bread, cubed
- 6 cups water
- 2 cups dried cannellini, rinsed and soaked overnight
- 1 ½ cups vegetable stock
- 1 tbsp. chopped fresh rosemary, plus 6 sprigs
- ¼ tsp. freshly ground black pepper
- 6 cloves garlic, chopped
- 3 peeled carrots, chopped
- 1 yellow onion, chopped
- 1 tsp. sea salt
- 1 bay leaf

## Directions
Make croutons:
- Heat 2 tablespoons extra virgin olive oil in a large frying pan set over medium heat; add chopped garlic and sauté for about 1 minute or until fragrant.
- Remove the pan from heat and let stand for at least 10 minutes to infuse garlic into oil.
- Discard the garlic and return the pan to heat.
- Add bread cubes to the pan and sauté, stirring regularly, for about 5 minutes or until lightly browned.
- Transfer the cooked bread to a bowl and set aside.
- Combine water, white beans, bay leaf and ½ teaspoon of sea salt in a soup pot set over high heat; bring the mixture to a rolling boil.
- Lower heat to low and simmer, partially covered, for about 75 minutes or until, beans are tender; drain the beans and reserve ½ cup of cooking liquid.
- Remove and discard bay leaf.
- Transfer the beans to a large bowl and set aside.

- In a separate bowl, combine ½ cup of cooked beans and the reserved cooking liquid; mash with a fork until smooth.
- Add the mashed beans into the remaining cooked beans and stir to mix well.
- Return the empty pot to heat and add the remaining extra virgin olive oil.
- Add onion and carrots; sauté for about 7 minutes or until carrots are crisp and tender.
- Stir in garlic quarters and sauté for about 1 minute or until fragrant.
- Stir in the bean mixture, stock, chopped rosemary, pepper and the remaining salt; bring to a gentle boil and then lower heat to low.
- Simmer for about 5 minutes or until stew is heated through.
- Ladle stew into bowls and sprinkle with croutons; garnish each serving with a rosemary sprig and serve.

# Cold Cucumber Soup

Total time: 20 minutes + Chilling time
Prep time: 20 minutes
Cook time: 0 minutes
Yields: 4 to 6 servings

## Ingredients
- Juice of 1 lemon
- ½ cup chopped fresh parsley
- 2 medium cucumbers
- 1 ½ cups low-sodium chicken broth
- 1 cup fat-free plain yogurt
- 1 1/2 cups fat-free half and half
- Salt and freshly ground black pepper, to taste
- Chopped fresh dill

## Directions
- In a blender or food processor, combine together lemon juice, parsley, and cucumbers and puree until smooth.
- Transfer half of the puree to a plate and set aside.
- Combine together yogurt, half and half, and broth in a medium-sized bowl.
- Add half of the yogurt mixture to the pureed mixture in the blender and puree again until well mixed.
- Sprinkle with salt and pepper and refrigerate in a container.
- Repeat the procedure with the remaining yogurt mixture and the puree.
- Stir the soup and garnish with fresh dill to serve.

# Curried Cauliflower Soup

Total time: 30 minutes
Prep time: 10 minutes
Cook time: 20 minutes
Yields: 4 to 6 servings

## Ingredients
- ⅓ cup raw cashews
- ¾ cup water
- 2 tsp. extra virgin olive oil
- 1 medium onion, diced
- 1 can (14-ounce) light coconut milk
- 1 large head cauliflower, chopped in small pieces
- ¼ tsp. ground cinnamon
- 1 tsp. evaporated cane sugar
- 1 tsp. ground turmeric
- 2 tbsp. curry powder
- ¼ cup chopped cilantro
- Caramelized onions
- Salt

## Directions
- Blend the cashews in a blender until finely ground.
- Add three-quarters of a cup of water to the cashews and continue blending for 2 more minutes.
- Strain the mixture through a fine mesh strainer into a bowl and set aside.
- Add olive oil to a large pot set over low heat.
- Sauté onions in the hot olive oil until golden brown.
- Add the cashew milk, coconut milk, cauliflower, cinnamon, sugar, turmeric, curry powder and salt.
- Add enough water to cover mixture and bring to a gentle boil.
- Lower the heat and simmer for about 10 minutes or until cauliflower is tender.
- Transfer the mixture to an immersion blender and blend to your desired consistency.
- Return to the pot and heat.
- Ladle the hot soup into bowls and serve garnished with cilantro and onions.

# Chicken and Lemon Soup

Total time: 25 minutes
Prep time: 10 minutes
Cook time: 15 minutes
Yields: 4 servings

## Ingredients
- 2 cans (14 ½ ounce) reduced-sodium chicken broth
- 1 small sliced carrot
- ½ cup long-grain white rice
- 1 finely chopped garlic clove
- ¼ cup freshly squeezed lemon juice
- ½ cup red bell pepper, thinly cut into small strips
- 2 cups chicken breast, cooked and cubed
- 1 tbsp. cornstarch
- 1 can (12 fluid ounce) fat-free evaporated milk, divided
- 2 tbsp. fresh basil, chopped

## Directions
- In a medium-sized saucepan, boil the broth.
- Add carrot and rice and cook for at least 10 minutes or until rice is tender.
- Stir in garlic, lemon juice, bell pepper and chicken.
- In a small bowl, combine together cornstarch and 1 tablespoon of evaporated milk; stir the mixture into the soup before gradually stirring in the remaining milk.
- Bring the mixture to a gentle boil.
- Remove the soup from heat and garnish with basil to serve.

# Moroccan Veggie Soup

Total time: 1 hour 5 minutes
Prep time: 20 minutes
Cook time: 45 minutes
Yields: 5 servings

## Ingredients
- 2 tbsp. olive oil
- 2 crushed garlic cloves
- 1 large roughly chopped yellow onion
- 2 tsp. ground cumin
- 1 tsp. ground coriander
- ¼ tsp. chili powder
- 500g peeled and sliced carrots
- 600g peeled and orange sweet potato
- 6 cups reduced-sodium chicken stock
- 300g can chickpeas, drained, rinsed
- ½ small lemon, juiced
- Sea salt and pepper, to taste
- Turkish bread croutons, for serving

## Directions
- In a saucepan, heat olive oil over medium high; sauté garlic and onions, stirring for about 3 minutes.
- Add cumin, coriander and chili powder; stir and let the mixture cook, stirring continuously for about 1 minute.
- Stir in carrots and sweet potato and cook, stirring for about 5 minutes.
- Add stock, cover and bring the mixture to a gentle boil.
- Lower heat to medium low and simmer, stirring frequently for about 20 minutes or until the vegetables are tender.
- Stir in chickpeas, cover and simmer for about 10 minutes or until the chickpeas soften.
- Working in batches, blend the soup in a blender until very smooth.
- Return the soup to the saucepan and reheat over medium low.
- Stir in 1 tablespoon of lemon juice, and salt and pepper to taste.

- Heat the soup, stirring constantly for about 30 seconds or until just heated through (do not boil).
- Divide among bowls, top with the croutons and sprinkle with ground pepper.
- Enjoy!

# Italian Bean Soup

Total time: 50 minutes
Prep time: 20 minutes
Cook time: 30 minutes
Yield: 4 servings

## Ingredients
- 1 tbsp. extra virgin oil
- 1 onion chopped
- 1 stalk celery, chopped
- 1 clove garlic, pressed
- 2 cans white kidney beans, washed and drained
- 1 can chicken broth
- 2 cups water
- ¼ tsp. freshly ground black pepper
- 1 pinch dried thyme
- 1 bunch fresh spinach, thinly sliced
- 1 tbsp. freshly squeezed lemon juice
- Parmesan cheese, grated, for topping

## Directions
- Heat oil in a large saucepan and add the onion and celery.
- Cook for about 8 minutes until tender.
- Add garlic and cook for a further 30 seconds.
- Slowly stir in the beans, broth, 2 cups of water, pepper and thyme.
- Bring to a boil; reduce the heat, and simmer for 15 minutes.
- Remove 2 cups of the bean mixture from soup and set aside.
- Blend the remaining soup until smooth and pour the blended soup back to the saucepan and stir in the beans you had set aside.
- Bring to a slow boil and add the spinach.
- Cook until wilted then add the lemon juice and remove from heat.
- Serve on four plates and top with grated Parmesan.

# Slow Cooker Stew

Total time: 10 hours 30 minutes
Prep time: 30 minutes
Cook time: 10 hours
Yield: 10 servings

## Ingredients

- 2 cups zucchini, cubed
- 2 cups eggplant, cubed
- 1 can tomato sauce
- 1 10oz package frozen okra, thawed
- 1 butternut squash, peeled, seeded and diced
- 1 cup onion, chopped
- 1 clove garlic, chopped
- ½ cup vegetable broth
- 1 carrot, thinly sliced
- 1 tomato, chopped
- ⅓ cup raisins
- ¼ tsp. paprika
- ½ tsp. ground cumin
- ½ tsp. ground turmeric
- ¼ tsp. ground cinnamon
- ¼ tsp. crushed red pepper

## Directions

Combine everything in a slow cooker, cover and cook for 10 hours or until vegetables are soft.

# Mediterranean Poultry Recipes

## Chicken Bruschetta

Total time: 30 minutes
Prep time: 10 minutes
Cook time: 20 minutes
Yield: 4 servings

### Ingredients
- 5ml olive oil, divided
- 1 boneless, skinless chicken breast
- 80g cherry tomatoes
- 5ml balsamic vinegar
- 10g fresh basil leaves
- 1 small cloves garlic, minced
- 1 small onions, chopped

### Directions
- Add half of the oil to the skillet and cook chicken over medium heat.
- In the meantime, cut basil leaves into slivers and prepare the vegetables.
- Heat the remaining oil and sauté garlic and onion for about 3 minutes.
- Stir in basil and tomatoes for about 5 minutes.
- Stir in vinegar
- Cook until heated through and serve the chicken topped with onion and tomato mixture.

# Coconut Chicken

Total time: 30 minutes
Prep time: 20 minutes
Cook time: 10 minutes
Yield: 4 servings

## Ingredients
- 20g coconut, shredded
- 30g almond flour
- 1 tsp. sea salt
- 1 small egg
- 100g chicken breast, boneless, skinless
- 7.5 ml coconut oil

## Directions
- In a bowl, combine shredded coconut, almond flour and sea salt.
- In a separate bowl, beat the egg; dip the chicken in the egg and roll in the flour mixture until well coated.
- Add coconut oil to a pan set over medium heat and fry the chicken until the crust begins to brown.
- Transfer the chicken to the oven and bake at 350°F for about 10 minutes.

# Turkey Burgers

Total time: 25 minutes
Prep time: 15 minutes
Cook time: 10 minutes
Yield: 4 servings

## Ingredients
- 1 large egg white
- 1 cup red onion, chopped
- ¾ cup fresh mint, chopped
- ½ cup dried bread crumbs
- 1 tsp. dill, dried
- ⅓ cup feta cheese, crumbled
- ¾ kg turkey, ground
- Cooking spray
- 4 hamburger buns, split
- 1 red bell pepper, roasted and cut in strips
- 2 tbsp. fresh lime juice

## Directions
- Lightly beat the egg white in a bowl and add onion, mint, breadcrumbs, dill, cheese, turkey and lime juice, mix well then divide the turkey mixture into four equal burger patties.
- Spray a large non-stick skillet with cooking spray and heat on medium-high setting.
- Carefully place the patties in the skillet and cook for 8 minutes on each side or according to preference.
- Once cooked, place the burgers on the sliced buns and top with pepper strips.

# Chicken with Greek Salad

Total time: 25 minutes
Prep time: 25 minutes
Cook time: 0 minutes
Yield: 4 servings

## Ingredients
- 2 tbsp. extra virgin olive oil
- ⅓ cup red-wine vinegar
- 1 tsp. garlic powder
- 1 tbsp. chopped fresh dill
- ¼ tsp. sea salt
- ¼ tsp. freshly ground pepper
- 2 ½ cups chopped cooked chicken
- 6 cups chopped romaine lettuce
- 1 cucumber, peeled, seeded and chopped
- 2 medium tomatoes, chopped
- ½ cup crumbled feta cheese
- ½ cup sliced ripe black olives
- ½ cup finely chopped red onion

## Directions
- In a large bowl, whisk together extra virgin olive oil, vinegar, garlic powder, dill, sea salt and pepper.
- Add chicken, lettuce, cucumber, tomatoes, feta, and olives and toss to combine well. Enjoy!

# Braised Chicken with Olives

Total time: 1 hour 50 minutes
Prep time: 20 minutes
Cook time: 1 hour 30 minutes
Yield: 4 servings

## Ingredients
- 1 tbsp. extra virgin olive oil
- 4 whole skinned chicken legs, cut into drumsticks and thighs
- 1 cup low-sodium canned chicken broth
- 1 cup dry white wine
- 4 sprigs thyme
- 2 tbsp. chopped fresh ginger
- 2 garlic cloves, minced
- 3 carrots, diced
- 1 medium yellow onion, diced
- 3/4¾ cup chickpeas, drained, rinsed
- ½ cup green olives, pitted and roughly chopped
- ⅓ cup raisins
- 1 cup water

## Dircctions
- Preheat your oven to 350°F.
- Heat extra virgin olive oil in a Dutch oven or a large ovenproof skillet over medium heat.
- Add the chicken pieces into the skillet and sauté for about 5minutes per side or until browned and crisped on both sides.
- Transfer the cooked chicken to a plate and set aside.
- Lower heat to medium low and add garlic, onion, carrots, and ginger to the same skillet; cook, stirring, for about 5 minutes or until onion is translucent and tender.
- Stir in water, chicken broth, and wine; bring the mixture to a gentle boil.
- Return the chicken to the pot and stir in thyme.
- Bring the mixture back the boil and cover.

- Transfer to the oven and braise for about 45 minutes.
- Remove the pot from the oven and stir in chickpeas, olives, and raisins.
- Return to oven and braise, uncovered, for 20 minutes more.
- Remove the skillet from oven and discard thyme.
- Serve immediately.

# Braised Chicken with Mushrooms and Olives

Total time: 45 minutes
Prep time: 10 minutes
Cook time: 35 minutes
Yield: 4 servings

## Ingredients
- 2 ½ pounds chicken, cut into pieces
- Sea salt
- Freshly ground pepper
- 1 tbsp. plus 1 tsp. extra virgin olive oil
- 16 cloves garlic, peeled
- 10 ounces cremini mushrooms, rinsed, trimmed, and halved
- ½ cup white wine
- ⅓ cup chicken stock
- ½ cup green olives, pitted

## Directions
- Heat a large skillet over medium-high heat.
- In the meantime, season the chicken with sea salt and pepper.
- Add 1 tablespoon of extra virgin olive oil to the heated skillet and add the chicken, skin side down; cook for about 6 minutes or until browned.
- Transfer to a platter and set aside.
- Add the 1 teaspoon of remaining extra virgin olive oil to the pan and sauté garlic and mushrooms for about 6 minutes or until browned.
- Add wine and bring to a gentle boil, reduce heat and cook for about 1 minute.
- Add the chicken back to the pan and stir in chicken broth and olives.
- Bring the mixture back to a gentle boil, reduce heat and simmer, covered, for about 20 minutes or until the chicken is cooked through.

# Chicken with Olives, Mustard Greens, and Lemon

Total time: 40 minutes
Prep time: 10 minutes
Cook time: 30 minutes
Yield: 6 servings

## Ingredients
- 2 tbsp. extra virgin olive oil, divided
- 6 skinless chicken breast halves, cut in half crosswise
- ½ cup Kalamata olives, pitted
- 1 tbsp. freshly squeezed lemon juice
- 1 1/2 pounds mustard greens , stalks removed and coarsely chopped
- 1 cup dry white wine
- 4 garlic cloves, smashed
- 1 medium red onion, halved and thinly sliced
- Sea salt
- Ground pepper
- Lemon wedges, for serving

## Directions
- Heat 1 tablespoon of extra virgin olive oil in a Dutch oven or large heavy pot over medium high heat.
- Rub the chicken with sea salt and pepper and add half of it to the pot; cook, for about 8 minutes or until browned on all sides.
- Transfer the cooked chicken to a plate and repeat with the remaining chicken and oil.
- Add garlic and onion to the pot and lower heat to medium; cook, stirring, for about 6 minutes or until tender.
- Add chicken (with accumulated juices) and wine and bring to a boil.
- Reduce heat and cook, covered, for about 5 minutes.
- Add the greens on top of the chicken and sprinkle with sea salt and pepper.
- Cook, covered, for about 5 minutes more or until the greens are wilted and chicken is opaque.
- Remove the pot from heat and stir in olives and lemon juice.
- Serve drizzled with accumulated pan juices and garnished with lemon wedges.

# Delicious Mediterranean Chicken

Total time: 55 minutes
Prep time: 25 minutes
Cook time: 30 minutes
Yield: 6 servings

## Ingredients
- 2 tsp. extra virgin olive oil
- ½ cup white wine, divided
- 6 chicken breasts, skinned and deboned
- 3 cloves garlic, pressed
- ½ cup onion, chopped
- 3 cups tomatoes, chopped
- ½ cup Kalamata olives
- ¼ cup fresh parsley, chopped
- 2 tsp. fresh thyme, chopped
- Sea salt to taste

## Directions
- Heat the oil and 3 tablespoons of white wine in a skillet over medium heat.
- Add the chicken and cook for about 6 minutes on each side until golden.
- Remove the chicken and put it on a plate.
- Add garlic and onions in the skillet and sauté for about 3 minutes and add the tomatoes.
- Let them cook for five minutes then lower the heat and add the remaining white wine and simmer for 10 minutes.
- Add the thyme and simmer for a further 5 minutes.
- Return the chicken to the skillet and cook on low heat until the chicken is well done.
- Add olives and parsley and cook for 1 more minute.
- Add the salt and pepper and serve.

# Warm Chicken Avocado Salad

Total time: 35 minutes
Prep time: 15 minutes
Cook time: 20 minutes
Yield: 4 servings

## Ingredients
- 2 tbsp. extra virgin olive oil, divided
- 500g chicken breast fillets
- 1 large avocado, peeled, diced
- 2 garlic cloves, sliced
- 1 tsp. ground turmeric
- 3 tsp. ground cumin
- 1 small head broccoli, chopped
- 1 large carrot, diced
- 1/3 cup currants
- 1 1/2 cups chicken stock
- 1 1/2 cups couscous
- Pinch of sea salt

## Directions
- In a large frying pan set over medium heat, heat 1 tablespoon extra virgin olive oil; add chicken and cook for about 6 minutes per side or until cooked through; transfer to a plate and keep warm.
- In the meantime, combine currants and couscous in a heatproof bowl; stir in boiling stock and set aside, covered, for at least 5 minutes or until liquid is absorbed.
- With a fork, separate the grains.
- Add the remaining oil to a frying pan and add carrots; cook, stirring, for about 1 minute.
- Stir in broccoli for about 1 minute; stir in garlic, turmeric, and cumin.
- Cook for about 1 minute more and remove the pan from heat.
- Slice the chicken into small slices and add to the broccoli mixture; toss to combine; season with sea salt and serve with the avocado sprinkled on top.

# Chicken Stew

Total time: 35 minutes
Prep time: 20 minutes
Cook time: 15 minutes
Yield: 4 servings

## Ingredients

- 1 tbsp. extra virgin olive oil
- 3 chicken breast halves (8 ounces each), boneless, skinless, cut into small pieces
- Sea salt
- Freshly ground pepper
- 1 medium onion, sliced
- 4 garlic cloves, sliced
- ½ tsp. dried oregano
- 1 ½ pounds escarole, ends trimmed, chopped
- 1 cup whole-wheat couscous, cooked
- 1 (28 ounces) can whole peeled tomatoes, pureed

## Directions

- In a large heavy pot or Dutch oven, heat extra virgin olive oil over medium high heat.
- Rub chicken with sea salt and pepper.
- In batches, cook chicken in olive oil, tossing occasionally, for about 5 minutes or until browned; transfer to a plate and set aside.
- Add onion, garlic and oregano, tomatoes, sea salt and pepper to the pot and cook for about 10 minutes or until onion is lightly browned.
- Add the chicken and cook, covered for about 4 minutes or until opaque.
- Fill the pot with escarole and cook for about 4 minutes or until tender.
- Serve the chicken stew over couscous.

# Chicken with Roasted Vegetables

Total time: 55 minutes
Prep time: 15 minutes
Cook time: 40 minutes
Yield: 2 servings

## Ingredients
- 1 large zucchini, diagonally sliced
- 250g baby new potatoes, sliced
- 6 firm plum tomatoes, halved
- 1 red onion, cut into wedges
- 1 yellow pepper, seeded and cut into chunks
- 12 black olives, pitted
- 2 chicken breast fillets, skinless, boneless
- 1 rounded tbsp. green pesto
- 3 tbsp. extra virgin olive oil

## Directions
- Preheat your oven to 400°F.
- Spread zucchini, potatoes, tomatoes, onion, and pepper in a roasting pan and scatter with olives.
- Season with sea salt and black pepper.
- Cut each chicken breast into four pieces and arrange them on top of the vegetables.
- In a small bowl, combine pesto and extra virgin olive oil and spread over the chicken. Cover with foil and cook in preheated oven for about 30 minutes.
- Uncover the pan and return to oven; cook for about 10 minutes more or until chicken is cooked through.
- Enjoy!

# Grilled Chicken with Olive Relish

Total time: 21 minutes
Prep time: 15 minutes
Cook time: 6 minutes
Yield: 4 servings

## Ingredients
- 4 chicken breast halves, boneless, skinless
- ¾ cup extra virgin olive oil, divided
- Sea salt
- Freshly ground black pepper
- 2 tbsp. capers, rinsed, chopped
- 1 ½ cups green olives, rinsed, pitted, and chopped
- ¼ cup lightly toasted almonds, chopped
- 1 small clove garlic, mashed with sea salt
- 1 ½ tsp. chopped fresh thyme
- 2 ½ tsp. grated lemon zest
- 2 tbsp. chopped fresh parsley

## Directions
- Heat grill to high heat.
- Place 1 chicken breast on one side of a plastic wrap and drizzle with about 1 teaspoon of extra virgin olive oil and fold the wrap over the chicken.
- Pound the chicken with a heavy sauté pan or a meat mallet to about ½ inch thick.
- Repeat the process with the remaining chicken and discard the plastic wrap.
- Sprinkle chicken with sea salt and pepper and coat with about 2 tablespoons extra virgin olive oil; set aside.
- In the meantime, combine ½ cup extra virgin olive oil, capers, olives, almonds, garlic, thyme, lemon zest and parsley in a medium bowl.
- Grill the chicken for about 3 minutes per side and transfer to a cutting board.
- Let cool a bit and cut into ½-inch-thick slices.
- Arrange the chicken slices on four plates and spoon over the relish.
- Serve immediately.

# Grilled Turkey with Salsa

Total time: 50 minutes
Prep time: 15 minutes
Cook time: 35 minutes
Yield: 6 servings

## Ingredients
### For the spice rub:
- 1 ½ tsp. garlic powder
- 1 ½ tsp. sweet paprika
- 2 tsp. crushed fennel seeds
- 2 tsp. dark brown sugar
- 1 tsp. sea salt
- 1 ½ tsp. freshly ground black pepper

### For the salsa:
- 2 tbsp. drained capers
- ¼ cup pimento-stuffed green olives, chopped
- 2 scant cups cherry tomatoes, diced
- 1 ½ tbsp. extra virgin olive oil
- 1 large clove garlic, minced
- 2 tbsp. torn fresh basil leaves
- 2 tsp. fresh lemon juice
- ½ tsp. finely grated lemon zest
- 6 turkey breast cutlets
- 1 cup diced red onion
- Sea salt
- Freshly ground black pepper

## Directions
- Mix together garlic powder, paprika, fennel seeds, brown sugar, salt and pepper in a small bowl.
- In another bowl, combine capers, olives, tomatoes, onion extra virgin olive oil, garlic, basil, lemon juice and zest, ¼ teaspoon sea salt and pepper; set aside.
- Grill the meat on medium high heat after dipping in the spice rub for about 3 minutes per side or until browned on both sides.
- Transfer the grilled turkey to a serving plate and let rest for about 5 minutes.
- Serve with salsa.

# Curried Chicken with Olives, Apricots and Cauliflower

Total time: 8 hours 50 minutes
Refrigerator time: 8 hours
Prep time: 15 minutes
Cook time: 35 minutes
Yield: 4 to 6 servings

## Ingredients

- 8 chicken thighs, skinless, boneless
- ¼ cup extra virgin olive oil, divided
- ½ tsp. ground cinnamon
- ¼ tsp. cayenne pepper
- 1 tsp. smoked paprika, divided
- 4 tsp. curry powder, divided
- 1 tbsp. apple cider vinegar
- Sea salt, to taste
- 1 head cauliflower, chopped
- 1 cup pitted green olives, halved
- ¾ cup dried apricots, chopped, soaked in hot water and drained
- ⅓ cup chopped fresh cilantro
- 6 lemon wedges

## Directions

- Combine chicken thighs, 2 tablespoons extra virgin olive oil, cinnamon, cayenne, ½ teaspoon paprika, 2 tablespoons curry powder, vinegar, and sea salt in a medium bowl; toss to coat and refrigerate covered, for about 8 hours.
- Position rack in the center of oven and preheat oven to 450°F.
- Prepare a rimmed sheet pan by lining it with parchment paper; add cauliflower and remaining olive oil, paprika, and curry powder; mix well.
- Add olives and apricots and spread the mixture in a single layer.

- Place the marinated chicken on top of the cauliflower mixture, spacing evenly apart, and roast in the preheated oven for about 35 minutes or until chicken is cooked through and cauliflower browns.
- Serve the cauliflower and chicken sprinkled with cilantro and garnished with lemon wedges.

# Chicken Salad with Pine Nuts, Raisins and Fennel

Total time: 10 minutes
Prep time: 10 minutes
Cook time: 0 minutes
Chill time: 1 hour
Yield: 1 large bowl

**Ingredients**
**For the dressing:**
- 1 tbsp. extra virgin olive oil
- 3 tbsp. mayonnaise
- ½ small clove garlic, mashed with sea salt
- Pinch cayenne
- 1 tbsp. freshly squeezed fresh lemon juice

**For the salad:**
- 3 tbsp. chopped sweet onion
- ⅓ cup small-diced fresh fennel
- 1 cup shredded cooked chicken
- 2 tbsp. golden raisins
- 2 tbsp. toasted pine nuts
- 2 tbsp. chopped fresh flat-leaf parsley
- Sea salt
- Freshly ground pepper

**Directions**
- Combine extra virgin olive oil, mayonnaise, garlic, cayenne, and lemon juice in a small bowl; mix well.
- In a separate bowl, mix onion, fennel, chicken, raisins, pine nuts, and parsley; gently add in the dressing and fold the ingredients together.
- Season with sea salt and pepper and refrigerate for at least 1 hour for flavors to meld before serving.

# Slow Cooker Rosemary Chicken

Total time: 7 hours 20 minutes
Prep time: 20 minutes
Cook time: 7 hours, 10 minutes
Yield: 8 servings

## Ingredients
- 1 small onion, thinly sliced
- 4 cloves garlic, pressed
- 1 medium red bell pepper, sliced
- 2 tsp. dried rosemary
- ½ tsp. dried oregano
- 2 pork sausages
- 8 chicken breasts, skinned, deboned and halved
- ¼ tsp. coarsely ground pepper
- ¼ cup dry vermouth
- 1 ½ tbsp. corn starch
- 2 tbsp. cold water

## Directions
- Combine onion, garlic, bell pepper, rosemary and oregano in a slow cooker.
- Crumble the sausages over the mixture, casings removed.
- Arrange the chicken in a single layer over the sausage and sprinkle with pepper.
- Add the vermouth and slow-cook for 7 hours.
- Warm a deep platter, move the chicken to the platter and cover.
- Mix the cornstarch with the water in a small bowl and add this to the liquid in the slow cooker.
- Increase the heat and cover.
- Cook for about 10 minutes.

# Chicken and Penne

Total time: 50 minutes
Prep time: 20 minutes
Cook time: 30 minutes
Yield: 4 servings

## Ingredients
- 1 package penne pasta
- 1 ½ tbsp. butter
- ½ cup red onion, chopped
- 2 cloves garlic, pressed
- ¾ kg chicken breasts, deboned and skinned, cut in halves
- 1 can artichoke hearts, soaked in water, chopped
- ½ cup feta cheese, crumbled
- 2 tbsp. lemon juice
- 1 tomato, chopped
- 3 tbsp. fresh parsley, chopped
- Sea salt
- Freshly ground black pepper
- 1 tsp. oregano, dried

## Directions
- Cook the penne pasta until al dente in a large saucepan with salted boiling water.
- Melt butter in a large skillet over medium heat and add the onions and garlic.
- Cook these for 2 minutes and add the chicken.
- Stir occasionally until the chicken is golden brown for about 6 minutes.
- Drain the artichoke hearts and add them to the skillet together with the cheese, lemon juice, tomatoes, oregano, parsley and drained pasta.
- Reduce the heat to medium low and cook for 3 minutes.
- Add the salt and pepper to taste and serve warm.

# Mediterranean Seafood Recipes

## Salmon and Vegetable Kedgeree

Total time: 30 minutes
Prep time: 10 minutes
Cook time: 20 minutes

### Ingredients
- 60ml basmati rice
- 7.5ml extra virgin olive oil
- 2g curry powder
- 100g skinless hot-smoked salmon portions, flaked
- 100g vegetable mix
- Sea salt and pepper, to taste
- 1 green onion, thinly sliced

### Directions
- In a saucepan of boiling salted water, add rice, turn heat to low and cook, covered, until just tender, for about 12 minutes.
- Add extra virgin olive oil to a pan set over medium heat and cook the onion, stirring until tender, for about 3 minutes.
- Stir in curry powder and continue cooking until fragrant, for about 1 minute.
- Stir in rice until well combined and then add salmon, vegetables, salt and pepper.
- Continue cooking until heated through, for about 3 minutes.
- Serve.

# Grilled Sardines with Wilted Arugula

Total time: 25 minutes
Prep time: 15 minutes
Cook time: 10 minutes
Servings: 4

## Ingredients
- 2 large bunches baby arugula, trimmed
- 16 fresh sardines, innards and gills removed
- 2 tsp. extra virgin olive oil
- Sea salt
- Freshly ground black pepper
- Lemon wedges, for garnish

## Directions
- Prepare your outdoor grill or a stove-top griddle.
- Rinse arugula under running water; shake off excess water and arrange them on a platter; set aside.
- Rinse sardines in water and rub to remove scales; wipe them dry and combine with extra virgin olive oil in a large bowl.
- Toss to coat.
- Place the sardines over the grill and grill for about 3 minutes per side or until golden brown and crispy.
- Season with sea salt and pepper and immediately transfer to the platter lined with arugula.
- Serve right away garnished with lemon wedges.

# Curry Salmon with Napa Slaw

Total time: 1 hour
Prep time: 15 minutes
Cook time: 45 minutes
Yield: 4 servings

## Ingredients

- 1 cup brown basmati rice
- A pinch of coarse salt
- A pinch of ground black pepper
- 1 pound (½ head) Napa cabbage, sliced crosswise
- 2 tbsp. extra virgin olive oil
- ¼ cup freshly squeezed lime juice
- ½ cup fresh mint leaves
- 1 pound carrots, coarsely grated
- 4 (6 ounces each) salmon filets
- 2 tsp. curry powder
- Lime wedges for serving

## Directions

- Bring two cups of water to a gentle boil in a large saucepan set over medium-low heat; add rice and season with sea salt and pepper; turn heat to low and cook, covered, for about 35 minutes.
- In the meantime, combine Napa cabbage, extra virgin olive oil, lime juice, mint, carrots, salt and black pepper in a large bowl; toss until well combined.
- Set broiler rack 4 inches from heat and preheat it.
- Place salmon in a baking sheet lined with foil and rub it with curry, salt and pepper.
- Broil the fish for about 8 minutes or until just cooked through.
- Serve the cooked rice alongside green salad and grilled salmon.

# Shrimp and Pasta

Total time: 20 minutes
Prep time: 15 minutes
Cook time: 5 minutes
Yield:  4 servings

## Ingredients
- 2 tsp. extra virgin olive oil
- 2 garlic cloves, minced
- 1 pound shrimp, peeled, deveined
- 2 cups chopped plum tomato
- ¼ cup thinly sliced fresh basil
- 2 tbsp. capers, drained
- ⅓ cup chopped pitted Kalamata olives
- ¼ tsp. freshly ground black pepper
- 4 cups hot cooked angel hair pasta
- ¼ cup crumbled feta cheese
- Cooking spray

## Directions
- In a large nonstick skillet set over medium high heat, heat extra virgin olive oil; add garlic and sauté for about 30 seconds.
- Add shrimp and sauté for 1 minute more.
- Stir in tomato and basil and lower heat to medium low; simmer for about 3 minutes or until the tomato is tender.
- Stir in capers, Kalamata olives and black pepper.
- In a large bowl, combine pasta and shrimp mixture; toss to mix and top with cheese.
- Serve immediately.

# Roasted Fish

Total time: 40 minutes
Prep time: 10 minutes
Cook time: 30 minutes
Yields: 4 servings

## Ingredients
- 1 tbsp. olive oil
- 1 (14-oz) can drained artichoke hearts
- 4 cloves garlic, crushed
- 1 green bell pepper, cut into small strips
- ½ cup halved pitted olives
- 1 pint cherry tomatoes
- 1 tbsp. fennel seed
- 1 ½ lb. cod, quartered
- 4 ½ tsp. grated orange peel
- 2 tbsp. drained capers
- ⅓ to ½ cup fresh orange juice
- A pinch ground pepper
- A pinch salt

## Directions
- Preheat your oven to 450°F.
- Generously grease a 10×15-inch baking pan with 1 tablespoon olive oil.
- Arrange the artichoke hearts, garlic, bell pepper, olives, tomatoes and fennel seed in the prepared pan.
- Place the fish over the vegetables and top with orange peel, capers, orange juice, pepper and salt.

# Baked Fish

Total time: 1 hour
Prep time: 10 minutes
Cook time: 50 minutes
Yields: 4 servings

## Ingredients
- 2 tsp. extra virgin olive oil
- 1 large sliced onion
- 1 tbsp. orange zest
- ¼ cup orange juice
- ¼ cup lemon juice
- ¾ cup apple juice
- 1 minced clove garlic
- 1 (16 oz.) can whole tomatoes, drained and coarsely chopped, the juice reserved
- ½ cup reserved tomato juice
- 1 bay leaf
- ½ tsp. crushed dried basil
- ½ tsp. crushed dried thyme
- ½ tsp. crushed dried oregano
- 1 tsp. crushed fennel seeds
- A pinch of black pepper
- 1 lb. fish fillets (perch, flounder or sole)

## Directions
- Add oil to a large nonstick skillet set over medium heat.
- Sauté the onion in the oil for about 5 minutes or until tender.
- Stir in all the remaining ingredients except the fish.
- Simmer uncovered for about 30 minutes.
- Arrange the fish in a baking dish and cover with the sauce.
- Bake the fish at 375°F, uncovered, for about 15 minutes or until it flakes easily when tested with a fork.

# Spanish Cod

Total time: 35 minutes
Prep time: 20 minutes
Cook time: 15 minutes
Yield: 6 servings

## Ingredients
- 1 tbsp. extra virgin olive oil
- 1 tbsp. butter
- ¼ cup onion, finely chopped
- 2 tbsp. garlic, chopped
- 1 cup tomato sauce
- 15 cherry tomatoes, halved
- ¼ cup deli marinated Italian vegetable salad, drained and chopped
- ½ cup green olives, chopped
- 1 dash cayenne pepper
- 1 dash black pepper
- 1 dash paprika
- 6 cod fillets

## Directions
- Place a large skillet over medium heat and add the olive oil and butter.
- Add the onion and garlic and cook until garlic starts browning.
- Add the tomato sauce and tomatoes and let them simmer.
- Stir in the marinated vegetables, olives and spices.
- Cook the fillet in the sauce for 8 minutes over medium heat.
- Serve immediately.

# Greek Salmon Burgers

Total time: 30 minutes
Prep time: 15 minutes
Cook time: 15 minutes
Yield:  4 servings

## Ingredients
- 1 pound skinless salmon fillets, diced
- 1 large egg white
- ½ cup panko
- 1 pinch sea salt
- ¼ tsp. freshly ground black pepper
- ½ cup cucumber slices
- ¼ cup crumbled feta cheese
- 4 (2.5-oz) toasted ciabatta rolls

## Directions
- In a food processor, combine together salmon, egg white, and panko; pulse until salmon is finely chopped.
- Form the salmon mixture into four 4-inch patties and season with sea salt and pepper.
- Heat the grill to medium high heat and cook the patties, turning once, for about 7 minutes per side or until just cooked through.
- Serve with favorite toppings (such as sliced cucumbers and feta) and buns.

# Grilled Tuna

Total time: 1 hour 16 minutes
Prep time: 10 minutes
Chill time: 1 hour
Cook time: 6 minutes
Yield: 4 servings

## Ingredients
- 4 tuna steaks, 1 inch thick
- 3 tbsp. extra virgin oil
- ½ cup hickory wood chips, soaked
- Sea salt
- Freshly ground black pepper
- Juice of 1 lime

## Directions
- Place tuna and the olive oil in a zip lock plastic bag, seal and refrigerate for an hour.
- Prepare a charcoal or gas grill.
- When using a coal grill, scatter a handful of hickory wood chips when the coals are hot for added flavor.
- Lightly grease the grill grate.
- Season the tuna with salt and pepper and cook on the grill for about 6 minutes, turning only once.
- Transfer to a plate.
- Drizzle the lime juice over the fish and serve immediately.

# Easy Fish Dish

Total time: 45 minutes
Prep time: 15 minutes
Cook time: 30 minutes
Yields: 4 servings

## Ingredients
- 4 fillets halibut (6 ounces)
- 1 tbsp. Greek seasoning
- 1 tbsp. lemon juice
- ¼ cup olive oil
- ¼ cup capers
- 1 jar (5 ounce) pitted Kalamata olives
- 1 chopped onion
- 1 large tomato, chopped
- A pinch of freshly ground black pepper
- A pinch of salt

## Directions
- Preheat your oven to 250°F.
- Arrange the halibut fillets onto an aluminum foil sheet and sprinkle with Greek seasoning.
- In a bowl, combine together lemon juice, olive oil, capers, olives, onion, tomato, salt and pepper; spoon the mixture over the fillets and fold the edges of the foil to seal.
- Place the folded foil onto a baking sheet and bake for about 40 minutes or until the fish flakes easily when touched with a fork.

# Salmon Bean Stir-Fry

Total time: 20 minutes
Prep time: 10 minutes
Cook time: 10 minutes
Yield: 4 servings

## Ingredients

- 1g crushed red pepper
- 2.5g cornstarch
- 5ml rice wine
- 7.5ml black bean-garlic sauce
- 7.5ml rice vinegar
- 30ml cup water
- 5ml canola oil
- 100g salmon, skinned, cubed
- 10g scallions, sliced
- 90g bean sprouts

## Directions

- In a bowl, whisk together crushed red pepper, cornstarch, rice wine, bean-garlic sauce, vinegar and water until well combined.
- Add oil to skillet set over medium heat.
- Stir in fish and cook for about 2 minutes.
- Stir in the sauce mixture, scallions and sprouts.
- Cook for about 3 minutes or until the sprouts are tender and cooked down.

# Mediterranean Flounder

Total time: 40 minutes
Prep time: 10 minutes
Cook time: 30 minutes
Yield: 4 servings

## Ingredients
- 5 Roma tomatoes
- 2 tbsp. extra virgin olive oil
- ½ onion, chopped
- 2 garlic cloves, chopped
- 1 pinch Italian seasoning
- 1 lb. flounder/tilapia/halibut
- 4 tbsp. capers
- 24 Kalamata olives, pitted and chopped
- 1 tsp. freshly squeezed lemon juice
- ¼ cup white wine
- 6 leaves fresh basil, chopped; divided
- 3 tbsp. Parmesan cheese

## Directions
- Preheat your oven to 425°F.
- Plunge the tomatoes into boiling water and immediately transfer them into a bowl of ice water; peel the skins and chop them
- Add extra virgin olive oil to a skillet set over medium heat and sauté onions until translucent.
- Stir in garlic, Italian seasoning, and tomatoes and cook until tomatoes are tender.
- Stir in wine, lemon juice, capers, olives, and half of basil.
- Lower heat and stir in Parmesan cheese; cook for about 15 minutes or until the mixture is bubbly and hot.
- Place fish in a baking dish and cover with the sauce; bake in the preheated oven for about 20 minutes or until fish is cooked through.

# Fish with Olives, Tomatoes, and Capers

Total time: 21 minutes
Prep time: 5 minutes
Cook time: 16 minutes
Yield: 4 servings

## Ingredients
- 4 tsp. extra virgin olive oil, divided
- 4 (5-ounce) sea bass fillets
- 1 small onion, diced
- ½ cup white wine
- 2 tbsp. capers
- 1 cup canned diced tomatoes, with juice
- ½ cup pitted black olives, chopped
- ¼ tsp. crushed red pepper
- 2 cups fresh baby spinach leaves
- Sea salt and pepper

## Directions
- Heat 2 teaspoons of extra virgin olive oil in a large nonstick skillet set over medium high heat.
- Add fish and cook for about 3 minutes per side or until opaque in the center.
- Transfer the cooked fish to a plate and keep warm.
- Add the remaining oil to the skillet and sauté onion for about 2 minutes or until translucent.
- Stir in wine and cook for about 2 minutes or until liquid is reduced by half.
- Stir in capers, tomatoes, olives, and red pepper and cook for about 3 minutes more.
- Add spinach and cook, stirring for about 3 minutes or until silted.
- Stir in sea salt and pepper and spoon sauce over fish.
- Serve immediately.

# Mediterranean Cod

Total time: 50 minutes
Prep time: 15 minutes
Cook time: 35 minutes
Yield: 4 servings

## Ingredients
- 1 tbsp. extra virgin olive oil
- 100g frozen chopped onion
- 1 tbsp. frozen chopped garlic
- 230g can Italian tomatoes, chopped
- 1 tbsp. tomato purée
- 400g pack skinless and boneless cod fillets
- 200g frozen mixed peppers
- 1 tbsp. chopped frozen parsley
- 50g pitted black olives
- 800g package frozen white rice

## Directions
- Add extra virgin olive oil to a saucepan set over medium heat; stir in onion and sauté for about 3 minutes.
- Add garlic and sauté for 2 minutes more or until fragrant.
- Stir in the tomatoes, tomato puree, and water and bring to a gentle boil.
- Reduce heat and simmer for about 20 minutes or until thickened.
- Add cod and peppers; nudge the fish in the sauce a bit and bring back to a boil; lower heat and simmer for about 8 minutes.
- Sprinkle with parsley and olives and simmer for 2 minutes more.
- In the meantime, follow package instructions to cook rice.
- Serve fish with hot rice.

# Grilled Salmon

Total time: 23 minutes
Prep time: 15 minutes
Cook time: 8 minutes
Yield: 4 servings

## Ingredients
- 2 tbsp. freshly squeezed lemon juice
- 1 tbsp. minced garlic
- 1 tbsp. chopped fresh parsley
- 4 tbsp. chopped fresh basil
- 4 salmon fillets, each 5 ounces
- Extra virgin olive oil?
- Sea salt and cracked black pepper, to taste
- 4 green olives, chopped
- Cracked black pepper
- 4 thin slices lemon

## Directions
- Lightly coat grill rack with olive oil cooking spray and position it 4 inches from heat; heat grill to medium high.
- Combine lemon juice, minced garlic, parsley and basil in a small bowl.
- Coat fish with extra virgin olive oil and season with sea salt and pepper.
- Top each fish fillet with equal amount of garlic mixture and place on the heated grill, herb-side down.
- Grill over high heat for about 4 minutes or until the edges turn white; turn over and transfer the fish to aluminum foil.
- Reduce heat and continue grilling for about 4 minutes more.
- Transfer the grilled fish to plates and garnish with lemon slices and green olives.
- Serve immediately.

# Mediterranean Meat Recipes

## Liver with Apple and Onion

Total time: 35 minutes
Prep time: 10 minutes
Cook time: 25 minutes
Yield: 2 servings

### Ingredients
- Extra virgin olive oil spray
- ½ lb. onion
- 2 Granny Smith apples
- 1 cup water
- 1 tbsp. fresh lemon juice
- 1 tbsp. white wine vinegar
- 1 tsp. brown sugar
- 1 tbsp. fresh rosemary, plus sprigs for garnish
- 2 tbsp. dried currants
- 2 tsp. unsalted butter
- 8 ounces calves' liver
- ¼ cup white wine
- ¼ tsp. sea salt
- olive oil spray

### Directions
- Preheat your oven to 200⁰F.
- Spray skillet with extra virgin olive oil spray and set over medium heat; add onions and sauté for about 4 minutes or until translucent.
- Add apples and cook for about 5 minutes or until they start to brown.
- Stir in water, lemon juice, vinegar and sugar and cook until apples are tender.
- Stir in rosemary and currants, cook, stirring for about 2 minutes and divide between two plates; keep warm in the oven.
- Melt butter in the same pan until frothing.
- Stir in liver and sauté for about 10 minutes or until browned on the outside.

- Divide the liver between the two plates of apple-onion mixture.
- Add white wine to the hot pan to deglaze; cook until the liquid is reduced by half and pour equal amounts over each serving.
- Serve garnished with fresh rosemary.

# Lamb Chops

Total time: 25 minutes
Prep time: 10 minutes
Cook time: 10 minutes
Standing time: 5 minutes
Yield: 4 servings

## Ingredients
- 1 tbsp. dried oregano
- 1 tbsp. garlic, minced
- ¼ tsp. black pepper, freshly ground
- ½ tsp. sea salt
- 2 tbsp. lemon juice, fresh
- 8 lamb loin chops, fat trimmed off
- Cooking spray

## Directions
- Preheat your broiler.
- In a small bowl, combine all the spices, herbs and lemon juice and rub this mixture on both sides of the lamb chops.
- Spray the broiler pan with the cooking spray and broil the lamb chops for 4 minutes on each side or depending on how done you want your chops.
- Cover the cooked lamb chops in foil and let them rest for 5 minutes and you are ready to serve.

# Sage Seared Calf's Liver

Total time: 30 minutes
Prep time: 20 minutes
Cook time: 10 minutes
Yield: 4 servings

## Ingredients
- 2 tsp. extra virgin olive oil
- 1 clove garlic, minced
- 8 ounces calves' liver, cut into small strips
- 1 tbsp. flat leaf parsley
- 1 tbsp. fresh sage
- 1 tsp. balsamic vinegar
- 2 tbsp. red wine
- 2 tsp. unsalted butter
- 1 tsp. fresh lemon juice
- ¼ tsp. sea salt
- Black pepper

## Directions
- Heat extra virgin olive oil in a nonstick skillet set over medium heat; stir in minced garlic and sauté for about 3 minutes or until translucent and fragrant.
- Add strips of liver, parsley and sage and cook for about 5 minutes or until the meat is seared on outside.
- Transfer the liver to a warm plate and quickly deglaze the pan with vinegar, red wine, butter, and lemon juice for about 30 seconds.
- Pour the sauce over the meat and serve right away.

# Seasoned Lamb Burgers

Total time: 30 minutes
Prep time: 20 minutes
Cook time: 10 minutes
Yield: 4 servings

## Ingredients
- 1 ½ pounds ground lamb
- 1 tsp. ground cumin
- ½ tsp. ground cinnamon
- 1 tsp. ground ginger
- ¼ cup extra virgin olive oil, divided
- 1 tsp. black pepper, freshly ground; divided
- ¼ cup fresh cilantro
- 2 tbsp. fresh oregano
- 1 small clove garlic, pressed
- ¾ tsp. red pepper flakes, crushed
- ¼ cup fresh flat leaf parsley
- 1 tbsp. sherry vinegar
- 2 pitas, warmed and halved
- Sliced tomato
- 1 8 oz of package plain Greek yogurt

## Directions
- Prepare a charcoal or gas grill fire.
- Mix the ground lamb with cumin, cinnamon, ginger, 1 tablespoon extra virgin olive oil and ½ teaspoon black pepper.
- Mix well and divide this into four burgers.
- Spray the grill with some olive oil and grill the burgers for 5 minutes on each side.
- Combine the rest of the olive oil, cilantro, oregano, garlic, red pepper flakes, parsley and vinegar in a food processor until it forms a thick paste.
- Serve each burger in pita bread on a plate with sliced tomato, the processed sauce and a serving of yogurt.

# London Broil with Bourbon-Sautéed Mushrooms

Total time: 1 hour, 15 minutes
Prep time: 15 minutes
Cook time: 60 minutes
Yield: 3 servings

## Ingredients
- ½ tsp. extra virgin olive oil
- ½ cup minced shallot
- ¾ lb. halved crimini mushrooms
- 6 tbsp. non-fat beef stock
- 3 tbsp. bourbon
- ½ tbsp. unsalted butter
- 1 tbsp. pure maple syrup
- Black pepper, to taste
- 1 lb. lean London broil
- ⅛ tsp. sea salt

## Directions
- Preheat your oven to 400°F.
- Heat a nonstick skillet in oven for about 10 minutes.
- Remove and add extra virgin olive oil; swirl to coat the pan.
- Stir in shallots and mushrooms until well blended; return to oven and roast the mushrooms for about 15 minutes, stirring once with a wooden spatula.
- Stir in beef stock, bourbon, butter, maple syrup and pepper; toss and return the pan to oven; cook for 10 minutes more or until liquid is reduced by half.
- Remove pan from oven and set aside.
- Place another nonstick skillet in the oven and heat for about 10 minutes.
- In the meantime, sprinkle salt and ground pepper over the steak and place it in the hot pan.
- Roast in the oven for about 14 minutes, turning once.
- Remove the meat from oven and warm the mushrooms.
- Place steak on a cutting board and let rest for about 5 minutes.
- Thinly slice beef and serve top with sautéed mushrooms to serve.

# Grilled Sage Lamb Kabob

Total time: 4 hours, 50 minutes
Marinating time: 4 hours
Prep time: 20 minutes
Cook time: 30 minutes
Yield: 2 servings

## Ingredients

- 1 tbsp. fresh lemon juice
- 2 tbsp. fresh chives
- 2 tbsp. fresh flat leaf parsley
- 2 tbsp. fresh sage
- 1 tbsp. dark brown sugar
- 1 tbsp. extra virgin olive oil
- 2 tbsp. dry sherry
- 1 tbsp. pure maple syrup
- ¼ tsp. sea salt
- 8 ounces lean lamb shoulder
- 2 cups water
- 4 medium red potatoes
- White onion, cut into halves
- 6 shitake mushroom caps
- ½ red bell pepper

## Directions

- In a blender, combine together lemon juice, chives, parsley, sage, brown sugar, extra virgin olive oil, sherry, maple syrup, and salt; puree until very smooth.
- Cut lamb into 8 cubes and add to a zipper bag along with the marinade; marinate in the refrigerator for at least 4 hours.
- Bring a pot with water to a rolling boil.
- Cut potatoes in halves and add to the pot along with half onion; steam for about 15 minutes. Remove from heat and let cool.
- Chop the remaining onion and pepper.
- On a skewer, alternate lamb cube, mushroom cap, pepper, onion and potato.
- Reserve the marinade.
- Grill the kabobs over hot grill, turning every 3 minutes and basting with the reserved marinade.

# Lemony Pork with Lentils

Total time: 45 minutes
Prep time: 15 minutes
Cook time: 30 minutes
Chill time: 8 hours
Yield: 4 servings

## Ingredients

- 2 tbsp. extra virgin olive oil, divided
- 4 (4 ounce) pork chops
- 2 tbsp. fresh lemon juice
- 1 tsp. lemon zest
- 1 clove garlic
- 2 tbsp. fresh rosemary
- 1 tbsp. parsley
- 1 tbsp. pure maple syrup
- 6 cups water, divided
- ½ cup green lentils
- 1 shallot
- 1 rib celery
- ½ cup dry sherry, divided
- 1 tsp. sea salt
- 1 tsp. unsalted butter
- ¼ tsp. red pepper flakes

## Directions

- In a zipper bag, combine extra virgin olive oil, pork chops, lemon juice, lemon zest, garlic clove, rosemary, parsley, and maple syrup; refrigerate for at least 8 hours.
- Combine 3 cups of water and green lentils in a saucepan set over medium heat and cook for about 20 minutes or until lentils are just tender; drain and rinse.
- Preheat your oven to 350°F.
- Heat a nonstick skillet over medium high heat and add the marinade; sear pork for about 2 minutes per side and transfer the skillet to the oven.
- In the meantime, heat 1 teaspoon of extra virgin olive oil to a second nonstick skillet set over medium high heat; add shallot, red pepper flakes and celery and lower heat to

medium; cook for about 4 minutes or until tender. Stir in lentils until warmed through.

- Add ¼ teaspoon sea salt and ¼ cup sherry and cook for about 2 minutes or until liquid is reduced by half. Stir in butter until melted.
- Divide the lentil mixture among four plates and top each serving with one pork chop from first skillet.
- Remove and discard garlic from marinade in the first skillet and deglaze the pan with ¼ cup sherry; increase heat and stir in ¼ teaspoon sea salt; cook until the liquid is reduced by half.
- Evenly pour the sauce over each serving and serve.

# Cumin Pork Chops

Total time: 30 minutes
Prep time: 10 minutes
Cook time: 20 minutes
Yield: 1 serving

## Ingredients
- 4-ounce lean center-cut pork chop
- ⅛ tsp. sea salt
- ⅛ tsp. ground cumin
- Olive oil spray
- 2 tbsp. mashed avocado
- 2 tsp. fresh cilantro leaves

## Directions
- Preheat your oven to 400°F.
- Heat a large skillet over medium heat.
- In the meantime, season pork chop with sea salt and cumin.
- Spray the pan with extra virgin olive oil and add the seasoned pork chop.
- Place the pan in oven and cook for about 10 minutes, turn the pork chop over and spread the seared part with avocado.
- Return to oven and cook for about 10 minutes more or until pork is done.
- Serve pork garnished with cilantro over mashed potatoes.

# Healthy Lamb Burgers

Total time: 40 minutes
Prep time: 10 minutes, plus 20 minutes resting time
Cook time: 10 minutes
Yield: 4 servings

## Ingredients
- 1 tbsp. extra virgin olive oil
- 1 lb. lean ground lamb
- 2 tbsp. yogurt cheese
- ⅛ tsp. ground allspice
- ½ cup cilantro leaves, chopped
- 1 small egg white
- 1 shallot, finely chopped
- 2 cloves garlic, chopped
- 2 tsp. fresh ginger, minced
- 1 red chili pepper, chopped
- ⅛ tsp. ground cumin
- 4 cardamom seeds
- ⅛ tsp. black pepper
- ¼ tsp. sea salt
- spray olive oil
- 4 whole-wheat hamburger buns

## Directions
- Mix together all the ingredients except spray olive oil and buns, and refrigerate for at least 20 minutes.
- Preheat your oven to 400° F.
- Heat extra virgin olive oil in a large nonstick skillet over medium heat.
- In the meantime, form lamb mixture into 4 burgers.
- Sear burgers in prepared pan for about 1 minute; transfer the pan to the preheated oven and cook for about 5 minutes, turn burgers over and cook for about 3 minutes more.

# Herb-Maple Crusted Steak

Total time: 25 minutes
Prep time: 15 minutes
Cook time: 10 minutes
Yield: 4 servings

## Ingredients
- 3 tbsp. rosemary
- 3 tbsp. fresh tarragon
- 3 tbsp. chives
- 3 tbsp. chopped oregano
- 4 tbsp. parsley
- 3 tbsp. maple syrup
- 4 (4 ounce) ribeye steaks, trimmed
- ½ tsp. sea salt
- ¼ tsp. black pepper
- spray olive oil

## Directions
- Preheat your oven to 450°F.
- Heat a nonstick skillet in the oven.
- In the meantime, combine the minced herbs on a plate
- Add maple syrup to a separate bowl.
- Season steak with sea salt and pepper and dip into the maple syrup; turn to coat well.
- Dip the steak into the herbs and turn to coat well. Repeat with the remaining steak.
- Remove the skillet from oven and spray with extra virgin olive oil; add steaks to the pan and turn until well seared.
- Return to oven and cook for about 4 minutes, turn and cook the other side for about 6 minutes more.

# Tenderloin with Blue Cheese Butter

Total time: 30 minutes
Prep time: 15 minutes
Cook time: 15 minutes
Yield: 2 servings

## Ingredients
- ⅛ tsp. black pepper
- 1 small shallot, minced
- 1 tsp. unsalted butter
- 2 tbsp. chopped parsley
- 2 tsp. blue cheese
- Extra virgin olive oil spray
- 2 4-ounce beef tenderloin filets
- ¼ tsp. sea salt

## Directions
- In a blender, blend together pepper, shallot, butter, parsley and blue cheese until very smooth.
- Preheat your oven to 450°F.
- Place a nonstick skillet in oven and spray with extra virgin olive oil.
- Season beef with sea salt and place in the pan; cook for about 7 minutes, turn over and cook the other side for about 4 minutes more.
- Transfer the meat to a plate and top with seasoned butter to serve.

# Green Curry Beef

Total time: 1 hour, 20 minutes
Prep time: 10 minutes
Resting time: 30 minutes
Cook time: 40 minutes
Yield: 3 servings

## Ingredients
- 1 tbsp. extra virgin olive oil
- ½ cup chopped parsley
- 1 cup cilantro leaves
- 1 white onion, chopped
- 1 fresh Thai green chili, chopped
- 2 cloves garlic, thinly sliced
- ¼ tsp. turmeric
- ½ tsp. ground cumin
- 2 tbsp. lime juice
- ¼ tsp. sea salt
- Black pepper
- 16 ounces beef top round, cut into small pieces
- 1 can light coconut milk
- 1/4 tsp. turmeric
- 1/2 tsp. ground cumin
- 1/4 tsp. sea salt

## Directions
Green curry paste:
- In a food processor or blender, combine extra virgin olive oil, parsley, cilantro, onion, chili pepper, garlic, turmeric, cumin, lime juice, sea salt, and pepper; process until very smooth.
- Combine beef and green curry paste in a bowl; toss to coat.
- Refrigerate for at least 30 minutes.
- When ready, heat a large skillet over medium high heat and add beef along with the green curry sauce.
- Lower heat and stir for about 10 minutes or until the meat is browned on the outside.
- Stir in coconut milk and cook for about 30 minutes or until the sauce is thick.
- Serve immediately.

# Roasted Pork with Balsamic Sauce

Total time: 1 hour
Prep time: 20 minutes
Cook time: 40 minutes
Yield: 6 servings

## Ingredients

- 1 tsp. extra virgin olive oil
- 1 clove garlic, minced
- ¼ cup diced yellow onion
- 1 ½ cups low-sodium vegetable or chicken broth
- ¼ cup balsamic vinegar
- ½ cup port
- ¼ cup dried cherries
- ½ cup 2% milk
- ¼ cup low-fat sour cream
- ¾ lb. pork tenderloin, trimmed

## Directions

- Heat extra virgin olive oil in a medium saucepan set over medium high heat; add garlic and onion and sauté for about 3 minutes or until tender.
- Stir in chicken broth, balsamic vinegar, port, and dried cherries and cook until the sauce is reduced to ½ cup.
- Scrape the sauce into the blender and blend until very smooth; stir in milk and sour cream and return to pan; stir until heated through.
- Preheat your oven to 375°F.
- Place pork tenderloin into a roasting pan and roast in the oven for about 15 minutes.
- Remove pork from oven and let rest for about 5 minutes and then slice into small slices. Serve the meat over 3 tablespoons of sauce.

# Mediterranean Beef Pitas

Total time: 15 minutes
Prep time: 10 minutes
Cook time: 5 minutes
Yield: 4 servings

## Ingredients
- 1pound ground beef
- Freshly ground black pepper
- Sea salt
- 1 ½ tsp. dried oregano
- 2 tbsp. extra virgin olive oil, divided
- ¼ small red onion, sliced
- 3/4cup store-bought hummus
- 2 tbsp. fresh flat-leaf parsley
- 4 pitas
- 4 lemon wedges

## Directions
- Form beef into 16 patties; season with ¼ teaspoon ground pepper, ½ teaspoon sea salt and oregano.
- Add 1 tablespoon of extra virgin olive oil in a skillet set over medium heat; cook the beef patties for about 2 minutes per side or until lightly browned.
- To serve, top pitas with the beef patties, hummus, parsley and onion and drizzle with the remaining extra virgin olive oil; garnish with lemon wedges.

# Parmesan Meat Loaf

Total time: 1 hour
Prep time: 10 minutes
Cook time: 50 minutes
Yield: 4 servings

## Ingredients
- 1½ pounds ground beef
- ½ cup bread crumbs
- ½ cup chopped flat-leaf parsley
- 1 grated onion
- 1 large egg
- ½ cup grated Parmesan
- ¼ cup tomato paste
- Sea salt
- Freshly ground black pepper

## Directions
- Preheat your oven to 400ºF. In a large bowl, mix together ground beef, bread crumbs, parsley, onion, egg, Parmesan cheese, tomato paste, sea salt and pepper.
- Line a baking sheet with foil and add the beef mixture, pressing to form an 8-inch loaf.
- Bake in the preheated oven for about 50 minutes or until cooked through.

# Mediterranean Flank Steak

Total time: 1 hour
Prep time: 20 minutes
Cook time: 40 minutes
Yield: 4 to 6 servings

## Ingredients
- 2 tbsp. chopped aromatic herbs (marjoram, rosemary, sage, thyme, or a mix)
- 2 cloves garlic, minced
- 2 tbsp. extra virgin olive oil
- 1 tbsp. sea salt
- 1 tbsp. ground black pepper
- 1½- to 2-lb. flank steak, trimmed
- ½ cup Greek vinaigrette

## Directions
- In a small bowl, mix together herbs, garlic, extra virgin olive oil, sea salt, and pepper; rub over the steak and let rest for about 20 minutes.
- In the meantime, heat your gas grill to medium high.
- Grill the steak for about 15 minutes, turning meat every 4 minutes for even cooking.
- Transfer the cooked steak to a cutting board and let rest for about 5 minutes; slice into small slices and place on plates.
- Drizzle with vinaigrette and serve immediately.

# Mediterranean Lamb Chops

Total time: 1 hour 30 minutes
Prep time: 30 minutes
Cook time: 1 hour
Yield: 4 servings

## Ingredients
- 2 tbsp. extra virgin olive oil, divided
- 3 garlic cloves
- 1 tsp. chopped fresh rosemary
- 2 tbsp. chopped fresh mint
- 4 lean lamb chops
- 2 yellow peppers, diced
- 2 red peppers, diced
- 4 zucchinis, sliced
- 1 eggplant, sliced
- 3 oz. crumbled feta cheese
- 9 oz. cherry tomatoes

## Directions
- Preheat your oven to 350°F.
- In a food processor, blend together 1 tablespoon extra virgin olive oil, garlic, rosemary, and mint until very smooth; smear over the lamb chops.
- On a baking sheet, mix peppers, zucchini, and eggplant; drizzle with the remaining oil.
- Place the lamb chops over the vegetables and roast in the preheated oven for about 25 minutes.
- Remove the baking sheet from oven and top with cherry tomatoes and feta cheese; return to oven and continue roasting for 10 minutes more or until lamb chops are cooked through and cheese begins to brown.
- Serve the roasted vegetables with lamb chops and green salad.

# Healthy Beef and Broccoli

Total time: 25 minutes
Prep time: 5 minutes
Cook time: 20 minutes

## Ingredients
- 8ml vegetable oil, divided
- 100g flank steak, thinly sliced
- 7.5g corn starch
- 90g broccoli florets
- 60ml water
- 1 green onion, thinly sliced
- 1/2 shallots, finely chopped
- 1 small cloves garlic, minced
- 1g crushed red pepper flakes
- 1g minced fresh ginger
- 5ml honey
- 20 ml soy sauce

## Directions
- Add oil to a skillet set over medium heat.
- Stir in beef and cook for about 8 minutes or until browned.
- Remove the beef from the pan and set aside.
- Add green onions, shallots and garlic to the same pan and cook for 1 minute, stirring.
- Stir in broccoli and cook for about 5 minutes.
- Combine cornstarch and water in a mixing bowl until well blended.
- In a separate bowl, combine red pepper flakes, ginger, honey, and soy sauce; stir in the cornstarch mixture until well combined.
- Add sauce to the pan and cook for about 5 minutes or until thick.
- Stir in beef and cook for about 3 minutes.
- Serve over brown rice.

# Mediterranean Pizza Recipes

## Mediterranean Veggie Pizza

Total time: 27 minutes
Prep time: 15 minutes
Cook time: 12 minutes
Yield: 4 servings

### Ingredients
- 1 tbsp. cornmeal
- 1 can refrigerated pizza dough
- 2 tbsp. commercial pesto
- ½ cup mozzarella cheese, shredded
- 1 pack frozen artichoke hearts, thawed, drained and coarsely chopped
- 1 ounce prosciutto, thinly sliced
- 2 tbsp. Parmesan, shredded
- 1 ½ cups Arugula leaves
- 1 ½ tbsp. fresh lemon juice
- Cooking spray

### Directions
- Preheat your oven to 500°F.
- Meanwhile, coat a baking sheet with cooking spray and sprinkle with cornmeal.
- Place the dough on the baking sheet by rolling it out.
- Evenly spread the pesto on the dough leaving out close to half an inch from the edge.
- Add the mozzarella over the pesto and now put the baking sheet on the bottom rack of the oven and bake for 5 minutes.
- Add the artichokes onto the pizza plus prosciutto and Parmesan then return the baking sheet to the oven and bake for another 5 – 6 minutes.
- In a small bowl, mix the arugula and the lemon juice and use this to top the pizza.
- You are ready to serve.

# Turkish-Style Pizza

Total time: 45 minutes
Prep time: 30 minutes
Cook time: 15 minutes
Yield: 1 14 by 9-inch pizza

## Ingredients
- 1 tsp. extra virgin-olive oil, plus 1 tbsp., divided
- Cornmeal, for dusting
- 12 ounces whole-wheat pizza dough
- 1 ½ cups grated Monterey Jack cheese or fontina
- 1 cup diced sweet onion
- 1 ½ cups diced tomatoes
- 2 tbsp. minced seeded jalapeno pepper
- 2 ounces sliced pastrami, diced
- Freshly ground pepper
- ⅓ cup fresh flat-leaf parsley, chopped

## Directions
- Position an inverted baking sheet on the lower oven rack and preheat to 500°F.
- Lightly oil a large baking sheet and dust with the cornmeal.
- Lightly flour a clean work surface and roll the dough into 10×15-inch oval.
- Transfer the rolled dough to the baking sheet and fold edges under to form a rim.
- Brush the rim with about 1 teaspoon of extra virgin olive oil.
- Sprinkle the crust with grated cheese, leaving about ½-inch border and top with onion, tomatoes, jalapeno, pastrami, and pepper.
- Drizzle with the remaining extra virgin oil and bake in the preheated oven for about 14 minutes or until the bottom is golden and crisp.
- Serve the pizza warm sprinkled with chopped parsley.

# Vegetarian Mediterranean Recipes

## Stewed Artichokes with Beans

Total time: 40 minutes
Prep time: 15 minutes
Cook time: 25 minutes
Yield: 4 servings

### Ingredients
- 1 ½ pounds fava beans, shelled
- 3 tbsp. freshly squeezed lemon juice
- 4 cups water
- 24 baby artichokes
- 1 lemon half, to rub artichokes
- 2 tsp. extra virgin olive oil
- 4 sprigs fresh flat-leaf parsley
- 4 sprigs fresh thyme
- 1/4 tsp. crushed red-pepper flakes
- 1/4 tsp. freshly ground black pepper
- 1 tsp. sea salt
- 3 peeled and lightly crushed cloves garlic
- 1 lemon half, to rub artichokes

### Directions
- Fill a large bowl with water and ice; set aside.
- Add water to a medium pot and bring to a rolling boil over high heat.
- Add fava beans and blanch for about 30 seconds.
- Remove the beans from hot water and add to a bowl with ice bath; let soak for about 5 minutes or until cold.
- Peel the skin from the fava beans and set aside.
- In a large bowl, combine lemon juice with 4 cups of water; set aside.
- Remove the tough outer leaves from the artichokes and cut off the tips.
- Trim each stem and peel; rub with the lemon half and place in the lemon-water mixture.
- Add extra virgin olive oil to a saucepan set over medium heat; heat until hot but not smoky.

- Add garlic, red pepper flakes, sea salt and black pepper; cook, stirring, for about 2 minutes or until the shallot is lightly browned.
- Stir in the artichokes, parsley, thyme, and 1 cup of lemon-water mixture; bring the mixture to a gentle simmer.
- Lower heat to medium low and continue simmering, covered, for about 14 minutes or until the artichokes are tender.
- Add the fava beans and continue cooking for 3 minutes more or until the beans are tender. Serve immediately.

# Mediterranean Pasta with Olives, Tomatoes and Artichokes

Total time: 35 minutes
Prep time: 15 minutes
Cook time: 20 minutes
Yield: 4 servings

## Ingredients

- 12 ounces whole-wheat spaghetti
- 2 tbsp. extra virgin olive oil, divided
- 2 garlic cloves, sliced
- ½ medium onion, thinly sliced lengthwise
- Coarse salt and ground pepper
- ½ cup dry white wine
- 1 artichoke heart, rinsed and cut lengthwise
- 1 pint grape or cherry tomatoes, halved lengthwise, divided
- ⅓ cup pitted Kalamata olives, cut lengthwise
- ½ cup fresh basil leaves, torn
- ¼ cup grated Parmesan cheese, plus more for serving

## Directions

- Cook pasta in a large pot of boiling salted water following package instructions, until al dente; drain and reserve 1 cup of pasta water.
- Return the cooked pasta to the pot.
- In the meantime, heat 1 tablespoon of extra virgin olive oil; add garlic and onion, season with sea salt and black pepper and cook, stirring regularly, for about 4 minutes.
- Stir in wine and continue cooking for about 2 minutes more or until the liquid is evaporated.
- Stir in the artichoke and continue cooking for about 3 minutes more or until starting to brown.
- Stir in half of the tomatoes, and olives and cook for 2 minutes.
- Add pasta and stir in the remaining olive oil, tomatoes, basil and cheese; Add the reserved pasta water, as desired, to coat the pasta.
- Serve immediately with extra cheese.

# Swiss Chard with Olives

Total time: 30 minutes
Prep time: 15 minutes
Cook time: 15 minutes
Yield: 4 servings

## Ingredients
- 1 ¼ pounds trimmed and rinsed Swiss chard
- 1 tsp. extra virgin olive oil
- 2 garlic cloves, sliced
- 1 small yellow onion, sliced
- 1 jalapeno pepper, chopped
- ⅓ cup Kalamata olives (brine-cured), pitted and roughly chopped
- ½ cup water

## Directions
- Separate stems from leaves of Swiss chard; cut the stems into small pieces and roughly chop the leaves; set aside.
- Heat extra virgin olive oil to a Dutch oven or a large skillet over medium heat.
- Add garlic, onion, and jalapeno; sauté for about 6 minutes or until onion is tender and translucent.
- Add olives, Swiss chard stems, and water and cook, covered, for about 3 minutes.
- Stir in the chard leaves and continue cooking, covered, for about 4 minutes or until the leaves and stems are tender.
- Serve immediately.

# Grilled Veggies Tagine

Total time: 1 hour
Prep time: 10 minutes
Cook time: 50 minutes
Yield: 6 servings

## Ingredients

- ¼ cup golden raisins
- 6 small red potatoes, cut in quarters
- ¼ cup pine nuts, toasted
- 2/3 cup couscous, uncooked
- 2 garlic cloves, pressed
- I medium red onion, wedged
- 1 tsp. fennel seeds, crushed
- ¼ tsp. cinnamon, ground
- 1 ¾ cups onions, chopped
- 1 tsp. extra virgin olive oil
- 1 tsp. cumin, ground
- ¼ cup green olives, pitted and chopped
- 1 ½ cups water
- ¼ tsp. freshly ground black pepper
- Cooking spray
- 2 red bell peppers, diced
- 1 green bell pepper, diced
- ½ tsp. kosher salt
- 2 tsp. balsamic vinegar
- ½ can tomatoes, chopped

## Directions

- Prepare a gas or charcoal grill.
- Combine the bell peppers, red onion, and ¼ teaspoon sea salt, vinegar and ½ teaspoon olive oil in a zip lock plastic bag and toss well.
- Place a large non-stick saucepan on medium heat and add the remaining olive oil and add the garlic and chopped onion.
- Sauté these for about 3 minutes and add fennel, cumin and cinnamon.
- Let them cook for a further 1 minute then add the remaining salt, olives, raisins, potatoes, tomatoes, black pepper and water and bring the pan to a boil.

169

- Cover the saucepan, and simmer for 25 minutes or until the potatoes are tender
- Remove the onions and bell peppers from the plastic bag and grill on a rack coated with cooking spray for about 10 minutes.
- Boil the remaining water in a separate saucepan and slowly stir in the couscous.
- Remove from heat and cover the pan and let it stand for 5 minutes.
- Serve the tomato mixture over couscous and top with the grilled onions, bell peppers and pine nuts.

# Chorizo Pilau

Total time: 50 minutes
Prep time: 10 minutes
Cook time: 40 minutes
Yield: 4 servings

## Ingredients

- 1 tbsp. extra virgin olive oil
- 1 large red onion, thinly sliced
- ¼ kg baby cooking chorizo, sliced
- 4 garlic cloves, minced
- 1 tsp. paprika, smoked
- 1 can tomatoes, chopped
- ¼ kg basmati rice
- 4 garlic cloves, minced
- ½ liter stock
- 1 small bunch parsley, chopped
- Zest of 1 lemon, peeled in thick strips and the remainder wedged
- 2 bay leaves, fresh

## Directions

- Place a thick saucepan on medium heat and pour in the oil.
- Add the onion and let it cook until golden brown for about 6 minutes.
- Push the onions to one side of the pan, pour in the chorizo and let it cook until it starts releasing some of its oils.
- The garlic and paprika are next.
- Stir for 2 minutes, then add the tomatoes and let cook for 5 minutes.
- Pour in the rice, lemon zest, bay leaves and stock.
- Stir everything in the pan and bring to a boil.
- Cover the pan and simmer for 12 minutes.
- Turn of the heat, take the lid off and cover the pan with foil, then put the lid back on and let it sit for about 15 minutes.
- Stir in the parsley and serve with lemon wedges.
- (Squeezing in the lemons gives the dish an amazing taste.)

# Pasta with Raisins, Garbanzos, and Spinach

Total time: 40 minutes
Prep time: 15 minutes
Cook time: 25 minutes
Yield: 6 servings

## Ingredients
- 8 ounces farfalle (bow tie) pasta
- 2 tbsp. extra virgin olive oil
- 4 garlic cloves, crushed
- ½ cup chicken broth (unsalted)
- ½ (19 ounces) can rinsed and drained garbanzos
- 4 cups chopped fresh spinach
- ½ cup golden raisins
- 2 tbsp. Parmesan cheese
- Cracked black peppercorns

## Directions
- Fill a pot ¾ full with salted water; bring to a rolling boil over high heat.
- Add pasta and cook for about 12 minutes or until al dente; drain and set aside.
- Heat extra virgin olive oil in a large skillet and sauté garlic until fragrant; add chicken broth and garbanzo beans and stir until warmed through.
- Stir in spinach and raisins and cook for about 3 minutes or until spinach is wilted.
- Divide pasta among plates and top each with about 1/6 of sauce, peppercorns and Parmesan.
- Serve right away.

# Eggplant Steak with Black Olives, Roasted Peppers, Chickpeas and Feta Cheese

Total time: 30 minutes
Prep time: 20 minutes
Cook time: 10 minutes
Yield: 4 servings

## Balsamic Marinade
- 2 cloves garlic, minced
- 1 tbsp. low-sodium tamari
- 1 tbsp. balsamic vinegar
- ¼ tsp. freshly ground black pepper
- 2 tbsp. extra virgin olive oil

## Eggplant Steaks
- 1 large eggplant, about 1 lb.
- ¼ lb. crumbled feta cheese
- 2 roasted red peppers, diced
- 1 ½ cups chickpeas, drained
- 4 tsp. balsamic vinegar
- Pinch of oregano
- ½ cup pitted black olives
- Sea salt
- Freshly ground black pepper
- 4 (6½-inch round) pita breads
- Fresh oregano, for garnish

## Directions:
Make marinade:
- In a bowl, combine marinade ingredients, gradually stirring in extra virgin olive oil until well combined.
- Set aside.
- Preheat your broiler or grill.
- Cut the eggplant into 4 ¼-inch-thick slices, lengthwise to look like steaks.
- Brush the eggplant slices with the marinade and broil or grill for about 2 minutes per side or until tender.
- Transfer the grilled eggplants to the plates, one on each.
- In a small bowl, combine feta, red peppers, chickpeas, oregano and black olives; season with sea salt and ground black pepper.

- Stir until well blended; stir in some marinade.
- Grill or toast pita bread and cut into wedges; set aside.
- Ladle about 2 scoops of the olive-pepper mixture onto eggplant "steak" and drizzle with balsamic vinegar.
- Add a few pita bread wedges and garnish with oregano sprigs.
- Repeat with the remaining ingredients and serve immediately.

# Tomato and Spinach Pasta

Total time: 35 minutes
Prep time: 10 minutes
Cook time: 25 minutes

## Ingredients
- 100g whole-wheat pasta
- 7.5ml extra virgin olive oil
- ½ onion, sliced
- 60g can tomatoes, drained
- 60g frozen spinach
- ⅓ cup crumbled feta cheese
- 1g salt
- 1g ground pepper

## Directions
- Follow package instructions to cook pasta in a pot of boiling water until al dente.
- In the meantime, add oil to a skillet set over medium heat; stir in onion and sauté for 3 minutes. Stir in tomatoes and simmer for about 10 minutes.
- Add spinach and cook until heated through.
- Drain the cooked pasta and toss with the sauce until well coated.
- Season with salt and pepper and serve topped with feta.

# Green Bean and Zucchini Sauté

Total time: 15 minutes
Prep time: 5 minutes
Cook time: 10 minutes
Yield: 4 servings

## Ingredients
- 7.5ml olive oil, divided
- 50g trimmed green beans - cut into small pieces
- ½ small zucchini, thinly sliced
- 2g red chili flakes
- 7.5ml lemon juice
- 15g sliced scallions
- 1g red chili flakes
- Handful of parmesan flakes
- 1g pepper
- 1g salt

## Directions
- Add half of the oil to a skillet set over medium heat.
- Stir in green beans, zucchini, salt and pepper and sauté, stirring, for about 9 minutes or until the vegetables are crisp tender.
- Remove the pan from heat and stir in lemon juice, scallions.
- Serve garnished with red chili flakes and cheese.

# Stuffed Grape Leaves Dish

Total time: 2 hours
Prep time: 30 minutes
Cook time: 1 hour 30 minutes
Yield: 8 servings

## Ingredients
- 30 fresh grape leaves
- 2 tbsp. extra virgin olive oil
- 2 cups finely diced onion
- 1 cup brown rice
- 1 cup dried currants or raisins
- 1 cup chopped fresh mint
- 1 cup chopped fresh parsley
- 1 cup chopped hulled pistachios
- 2 cups tomato juice
- Sea salt and pepper, to taste
- Pomegranate molasses, to drizzle
- ¼ cup freshly squeezed lemon juice
- 1 lemon, sliced
- 1 tsp. extra virgin olive oil for brushing casserole dish and top of casserole

## Directions
- Place grape leaves in a pot of boiling water; cook for about 2 minutes and remove from heat; drain, and set aside.
- In a large saucepan set over medium heat, heat extra virgin olive oil; add onion, and sauté for about 10 minutes or until lightly browned.
- Stir in rice and 2 ½ cups of water; bring to a gentle boil, cover and reduce heat to medium low.
- Cook for about 40 minutes or until rice is cooked through and water is absorbed.
- Remove the cooked rice from heat and stir in lemon juice, raisins, mint, parsley, pistachios, tomato juice, sea salt, and pepper.
- Preheat your oven to 350°F.
- Grease a 2-quart baking dish with extra virgin olive oil and line its bottom with grape leaves, allowing them to hang over the sides.

- With paper towels, pat the leaves dry and spread with half of the rice mixture.
- Top the rice mixture with more grape leaves and top with the remaining rice.
- Cover with the remaining leaves and fold over the leaves around edges to seal.
- Brush the top with extra virgin olive oil and bake in the preheated oven for about 40 minutes or until casserole is firm and dry and the grape leaves darken.
- Using a wet knife, cut the casserole into eight pieces and place each on eight plates.
- Drizzle each serving with pomegranate molasses and garnish with lemon slices.

# Olive, Bell Pepper and Arugula Salsa

Total time: 30 minutes
Prep time: 25 minutes
Cook time: 5 minutes
Yield: 1 ½ cups

## Ingredients
- 1 ½ tbsp. extra virgin olive oil
- 1 tsp. crushed fennel seeds
- 1 red and 1 yellow bell peppers, diced
- 16 pitted Kalamata olives, chopped
- Sea salt and pepper, to taste
- ½ cup chopped baby arugula

## Directions
- In a large nonstick skillet, heat extra virgin olive oil; sauté fennel seeds for about 1 minute, stirring.
- Stir in bell peppers and continue sautéing for 4 minutes more or until peppers are tender.
- Scrape the pepper mixture into a bowl; stir in olives, sea salt, and pepper.
- Let stand for at least 2 minutes, stirring occasionally, for flavors to meld.
- Add in arugula, toss until slightly wilted, and serve.

# Roasted Pepper and Bean Dip

Total time: 10 minutes
Prep time: 10 minutes
Cook time: 0 minutes
Yield: 2 ½ Cups

## Ingredients
- 1 (7-oz.) jar roasted red bell peppers
- 1 tbsp. extra virgin olive oil
- 1 16-oz. can cannellini beans, rinsed, drained
- 1 cup (6 oz.) light firm silken tofu
- 1 clove garlic, chopped
- ½ tsp. ground cumin
- 2 tbsp. freshly squeezed lime juice
- ⅓ cup cilantro leaves
- ½ tsp. sea salt

## Directions
- Set aside ¼ cup of roasted peppers.
- Place the remaining roasted peppers in a food processor along with other ingredients; process until very smooth.
- Spoon the pepper mixture into a serving bowl; stir the reserved peppers into the mixture. Serve at room temperature or chilled.

# Mediterranean Wrap

Total time: 35 minutes
Prep time: 25 minutes
Cook time: 10 minutes
Yield: 4 servings

## Ingredients
- ½ kg fresh mushrooms, chopped
- 1 eggplant, sliced
- 1 zucchini, sliced
- 1 red onion, sliced
- 1 red bell pepper, sliced
- 1 tbsp. extra virgin olive oil
- Salt and pepper to taste
- ⅓ cup basil pesto
- 4 whole grain tortillas
- ¼ cup goat cheese
- 1/3 cup basil pesto
- 1 avocado, sliced

## Directions
- Place the mushrooms, eggplant, zucchini, onion and bell pepper into a container with a tight fitting lid.
- Add the olive oil, salt and pepper and cover with lid then shake well.
- Heat a skillet and pour in the seasoned vegetables on medium heat and cook for 10 minutes, stirring regularly.
- Spread 1 tablespoon of goat cheese and pesto on each tortilla.
- Add the avocado and top with the cooked vegetables.
- Fold in the bottom of each tortilla and roll into a wrap.

# Vegan Bruschetta

Total time: 10 minutes
Prep time: 5 minutes
Cook time: 5 minutes
Yields: 12 servings

## Ingredients
- 1 tsp. balsamic vinegar
- ½ tsp. minced garlic
- 2 tomatoes, sliced
- A pinch of ground black pepper
- 8 fresh basil leaves
- 12 (½ inch) slices Italian bread

## Directions
- Combine together all the topping ingredients and spread evenly over each bread slice.
- Toast at 375 °F for a few minutes or until crisp.
- Enjoy!

# Mediterranean Appetizers

## Feta and Greek Yogurt Dip

Total time: 10 minutes
Prep time: 10 minutes
Cook time: 0 minutes
Yields: 8 servings

### Ingredients
- ¼ cup crumbled tomato-basil feta cheese
- 2 tbsp. reduced-fat mayonnaise
- 1 (6-oz) container Greek fat-free plain yogurt
- 2 tbsp. fresh parsley, chopped
- Assorted fresh vegetables

### Directions
- Mix together cheese, mayonnaise, yogurt and parsley in a small bowl until well blended.
- Divide the dip among bowls and serve with your favorite vegetables.

# Eggplant and Olive Dip

Total time: 40 minutes
Prep time: 15 minutes
Cook time: 25 minutes
Yield: Approximately 2 Cups

## Ingredients
- 2 (10 ounces each) Italian eggplants, cut into halves lengthwise
- 1 ½ tsp. extra virgin olive oil, divided
- ½ cup pitted green olives, such as Sicilian or Picholine
- ½ cup pitted Kalamata olives
- Pinch of red-pepper flakes
- 1 tsp. finely grated lemon zest
- 1 garlic clove, thinly sliced
- 1/4 tsp. coarse salt
- 1 tsp. fresh oregano, finely chopped
- Small oregano leaves for garnish
- Long zest strips for garnish
- 2 yellow bell peppers, ribs and seeds removed, diced

## Directions
- Preheat your oven to 400°F.
- Arrange the eggplants, cut-side down, on a baking sheet and brush with ½ teaspoon of extra virgin olive oil.
- Spread garlic on top and season with sea salt; roast in the preheated oven for about 20 minutes or until tender and golden.
- Remove from heat and let cool for at least 5 minutes.
- Remove and discard the eggplant seeds and spoon the flesh into a food processor, along with garlic; pulse until smooth and transfer to a bowl.
- Add the olives to the processor and process until roughly chopped; add to the eggplant mixture and stir in the remaining extra virgin olive oil, red pepper flakes, lemon zest, and the chopped oregano.
- Garnish with lemon zest strips and fresh oregano leaves and serve with bell peppers.

# Lemony Garlic and Sesame Hummus

Total time: 5 minutes
Prep time: 5 minutes
Cook time: 0 minutes
Yield: Approximately 3 ½ cups

## Ingredients
- 2 tbsp. toasted white sesame seeds
- 2 tbsp. extra virgin olive oil
- 3 peeled and crushed garlic cloves
- 15 ounces drained garbanzo beans, liquid reserved
- 2 tbsp. freshly squeezed lemon juice
- 2 tbsp. tahini
- 1 ½ tbsp. minced lemon peel
- 1 tbsp. minced orange peel
- Sea salt
- White pepper

## Directions
- Combine sesame seeds, extra virgin olive oil, garlic, garbanzo beans (reserve 1 tablespoon for garnish), lemon juice, and tahini in a food processor; process, adding garbanzo bean liquid if necessary until you achieve desired consistency.
- Season hummus with sea salt and pepper and transfer to a serving bowl.
- Garnish with the reserved beans and sprinkle with lemon and orange peel.
- Refrigerate, tightly covered, until chilled. Enjoy!

# Warm Lemon Rosemary Olives

Total time: 35 minutes
Prep time: 5 minutes
Cook time: 30 minutes
Yields: 12 servings

## Ingredients
- 1 tsp. crushed red pepper flakes
- 2 sprigs fresh rosemary
- 3 cups mixed olives
- 1 tsp. grated lemon peel
- 1 tsp. olive oil
- Lemon twists, optional

## Directions
- Preheat your oven to 400°F.
- Place pepper flakes, rosemary, olives and grated lemon peel onto a large sheet of foil; drizzle with oil and fold the foil.
- Pinch the edges of the sheet to tightly seal.
- Bake in the preheated oven for about 30 minutes.
- Remove from the sheet and place the mixture to serving dish.
- Serve warm garnished with lemon twists.

# Creamy Cucumbers

Total time: 15 minutes
Prep time: 15 minutes
Cook time: 0 minutes
Yield: 4 servings

## Ingredients
- 2 English cucumbers, thinly sliced
- 1 ½ cups low-fat Greek yogurt
- 2 tbsp. lemon juice, fresh
- 1 ½ tsp. mustard seeds
- Coarse salt and ground pepper, to taste
- Small bunch dill

## Directions
Combine all the ingredients in a bowl until well combined.

# Roasted Veggie Hummus

Total time: 1 hour
Prep time: 20 minutes
Cook time: 40 minutes
Yields: 20 servings

## Ingredients
- 1 bulb garlic
- ¾ cup olive oil, divided
- 1 egg plant, halved
- 1 red bell pepper, halved
- ⅓ cup lemon juice, freshly squeezed
- 2 cans chickpeas, drained
- ¼ cup sesame tahini paste
- ⅓ tsp. smoked paprika
- ½ tsp. salt

## Direction
- Heat your oven to 450°F and line a baking pan with foil.
- Cut the very top of the garlic bulb off and drizzle with 1 teaspoon of olive oil.
- Next wrap it up in foil.
- On a separate pan, place the eggplant and bell pepper, drizzle with 2 tablespoons of olive oil, and toss so it coats evenly.
- Place the wrapped garlic into the pan containing the vegetables.
- Roast for 30 minutes without covering and cool for 10 minutes.
- Remove the peels from eggplant and bell pepper and chop the vegetables into small pieces.
- Place the chickpeas in a food processor with a metal blade and process until smooth.
- Next, squeeze the pulp from the garlic into the processor; add all the other ingredients including the roasted vegetables and process until well blended.
- Serve into small serving bowls and serve immediately and refrigerate the remainder.

# Healthy Nachos

Total time: 12 minutes
Prep time: 10 minutes
Cook time: 2 minutes
Yields: 6 servings

## Ingredients
- 1 medium green onion, thinly sliced (about 1 tbsp.)
- 1 finely chopped and drained plum tomato
- 2 tsp. oil from container of sun-dried tomatoes
- 2 tbsp. sun-dried tomatoes in oil, finely chopped
- 2 tbsp. Kalamata olives, finely chopped
- 4 oz. restaurant-style corn tortilla chips
- 1 (4-oz) package finely crumbled feta cheese

## Directions
- Mix together onion, plum tomato, oil, sun-dried tomatoes and olives in a small bowl; set aside.
- Arrange the tortillas chips on a microwavable plate in a single layer; evenly top with cheese and microwave on high for 1 minute.
- Rotate the plate half turn and continue microwaving for 30 more seconds or until cheese is bubbly.
- Evenly spread the tomato mixture over the chips and cheese and serve.

# Jalapeno Boats

Total time: 35 minutes
Prep time: 10 minutes
Cook time: 25 minutes
Yields: 44 servings

## Ingredients
- 1 bag (12 oz.) vegetarian burger crumbles
- 1 cup Parmesan cheese, shredded
- 1 package (8 oz.) softened light cream cheese
- 22 large jalapeno peppers, cut into halves lengthwise and seeds removed

## Directions
- Sauté crumbles in a large skillet set over medium heat for about 5 minutes or until heated through.
- Combine together shredded Parmesan and softened cream cheese in a small bowl; fold in the crumble.
- Preheat oven to 425°F. Spoon about 1 tablespoon of the crumble-cheese mixture into each jalapeno half; arrange the jalapeno halves on a baking sheet, cheese side up, and bake in preheated oven for about 20 minutes or until the filling is bubbly and lightly browned.

# Greek Potatoes

Total time: 2 hours 20 minutes
Prep time: 20 minutes
Cook time: 2 hours
Yields: 4 servings

## Ingredients
- ¼ cup fresh lemon juice
- 2 finely chopped cloves garlic
- 1 ½ cups water
- ⅓ cup olive oil
- A pinch of ground black pepper
- 2 cubes chicken bouillon
- 1 tsp. dried rosemary
- 1 tsp. dried thyme
- 6 peeled and quartered potatoes

## Directions
- Preheat your oven to 350°F.
- Mix together lemon juice, garlic, water, olive oil, pepper, bouillon cubes, rosemary and thyme in a small bowl.
- Arrange the potatoes in a single layer in a medium-sized baking dish and top with olive oil mixture.
- Bake covered, turning twice, for about 2 hours or until tender.

# Stuffed Celery Bites

Yields: 8 servings
Total time: 19 minutes
Prep time: 15 minutes
Cook time: 4 minutes
Resting time: 4 hours

## Ingredients
- Olive oil cooking spray
- 1 clove garlic, minced
- 2 tbsp. pine nuts
- 8 stalks celery
- Celery leaves
- ¼ cup Italian cheese blend, shredded
- 1 (8-ounce) fat-free cream cheese
- 2 tbsp. sunflower seeds, dry-roasted

## Directions
- Coat a nonstick skillet with olive oil cooking spray; add garlic and pine nuts and sauté over medium heat for about 4 minutes or until the nuts are golden brown.
- Set aside.
- Cut off the wide base and tops from celery and remove 2 thin strips from the round side of celery to create a flat surface.
- Combine Italian cheese and cream cheese in a bowl; spread into celery and cut each celery stalk into 2-inch pieces.
- Sprinkle half of the celery pieces with sunflower seeds and half with the pine nut mixture; cover and let stand for at least 4 hours before serving.

# Pesto-Stuffed Mushrooms

Total time: 6 hours 15 minutes
Prep time: 15 minutes
Cook (Dehydrating) time: 6 hours
Yields: 14 servings

## Ingredients:

- 14+ button mushrooms, washed and stemmed
- ½ cup extra virgin olive oil
- 3 cloves garlic
- 2 cups basil
- ½ cup pine nuts
- 1 cup walnuts
- ½ tsp. sea salt

## Directions:

- Arrange the mushroom caps top-side down on a plate.
- In a food processor, blend together stuffing ingredients until very smooth.
- Scoop an equal amount of the stuffing into each cap and dehydrate at 105°F until soft, for about 6 hours.
- Serve warm.

# Squash Fries

Total time: 25 minutes
Prep time: 15 minutes
Cook time: 10 minutes
Yields: 6 servings

## Ingredients
- 1 medium butternut squash
- 1 tbsp. extra virgin olive oil
- ½ tbsp. Grapeseed oil?
- ⅛ tsp. sea salt
-
-

## Directions
- Peel and remove seeds from the squash; cut into thin slices and place them in a bowl.
- Coat with extra virgin olive oil and grapeseed oil; sprinkle with salt and toss to coat well.
- Arrange the squash slices onto three baking sheets and broil in the oven until crispy.

# Roasted Balsamic Beets

Total time: 1 hour 30 minutes
Prep time: 15 minutes
Cook time: 1 hour 15 minutes
Yields: 4 servings

## Ingredients
- 3-4 medium beets
- 2 tbsp. extra virgin olive oil
- 1 tbsp. balsamic vinegar
- ½ tsp. sea salt

## Directions
- Scrub the beets and wash well; cut into 6 wedges and place them in a baking dish.
- Drizzle the beets with extra virgin olive oil, vinegar, and salt and bake, covered, at 375°F for about 1 hour.
- Uncover and continue baking for 15 more minutes or until almost tender.

# Fig Tapenade

Total time: 15 minutes
Prep time: 15 minutes
Cook time: 0 minutes
Yields: 16 servings

## Ingredients
- 1 cup dried figs
- ½ cup water
- 1 cup Kalamata olives
- 1 tbsp. chopped fresh thyme
- ½ tsp. balsamic vinegar
- 1 tbsp. extra virgin olive oil

## Directions
- Pulse the figs in a food processor until well chopped; add water and continue pulsing to form a paste. Add olives and pulse until well blended.
- Add thyme, vinegar, and extra virgin olive oil and pulse until very smooth.
- Serve with walnut crackers.

# Healthy Spiced Nuts

Total time: 20 minutes
Prep time: 10 minutes
Cook time: 10 minutes
Yields: 4 servings

## Ingredients
- ⅔ cup walnuts
- ⅔ cup pecans
- ⅔ cup almonds
- ½ tsp. black pepper
- ½ tsp. cumin
- 1 tsp. chili powder
- ½ tsp. sea salt
- 1 tbsp. extra virgin olive oil

## Directions
- Put the nuts in a skillet set over medium heat and toast until lightly browned.
- In the meantime, prepare the spice mixture; combine black pepper, cumin, chili powder, and salt in a bowl.
- Coat the toasted nuts with extra virgin olive oil and sprinkle with the spice mixture to serve.

# Roasted Sweet Potato Chips

Total time: 1 hour 15 minutes
Prep time: 15 minutes
Cook time: 1 hour
Yields: 1 to 2 servings

## Ingredients
- 1 large sweet potato
- 1 tbsp. extra virgin olive oil
- Salt

## Directions
- Preheat your oven to 300°F.
- Scrub potato and slice into thin slices.
- Toss together the potato slices with salt and extra virgin olive oil in a bowl; arrange them in a single layer on a cookie sheet.
- Bake for about 1 hour, flipping every 15 minutes, until crispy and browned.

# Roasted Asparagus

Total time: 15 minutes
Prep time: 5 minutes
Cook time: 10 minutes
Yield: 4 servings

## Ingredients
- 1 pound fresh asparagus
- 1 tbsp. extra virgin olive oil
- 1 medium lemon
- 1/2 tsp. freshly grated nutmeg
- 1/2 tsp. kosher salt
- ½ tsp. black pepper

## Directions
- Preheat your oven to 500°F.
- Arrange asparagus on an aluminum foil and drizzle with extra virgin olive oil; toss until well coated.
- Spread the asparagus in a single layer and fold the edges of foil to make a tray.
- Roast the asparagus in the oven for about 5 minutes; toss and continue roasting for 5 minutes more or until browned.
- Sprinkle the roasted asparagus with nutmeg, salt, zest and pepper to serve.

# Delicious Greek Yogurt Dip

Total time: 10 minutes
Prep time: 10 minutes
Cook time: 0 minutes
Yield: 2 servings

## Ingredients
- 1 tbsp. extra virgin olive oil
- 1 tbsp. red wine vinegar
- 2 garlic gloves, sliced
- ¼ tsp. sea salt
- 1 tbsp. chopped fresh dill weed
- 1 tbsp. chopped fresh mint leaves
- 1 cup nonfat plain Greek yogurt
- 1 green onion, sliced
- 1 tbsp. pomegranate seeds

## Directions
- Mix together extra virgin olive oil, vinegar, garlic, sea salt, dill, mint and Greek yogurt in a small bowl.
- To serve, garnish with onion slices and pomegranate seeds.

# Mediterranean Hummus Nachos

Total time: 24 minutes
Prep time: 20 minutes
Cook time: 4 minutes
Yield: 8 servings

## Ingredients
- 4 cups salted pita chips
- 1 (8 oz.) container roasted red pepper hummus
- ¼ cup chopped pitted Kalamata olives
- 1 plum (Roma) tomato, seeded, chopped
- ½ cup chopped cucumber
- 1 tbsp. chopped fresh oregano leaves
- 1/4 cup crumbled feta cheese
- 1 tsp. finely shredded lemon peel

## Directions
- Preheat your oven to 400°F.
- In a single layer, arrange the pita chips on a heatproof platter and drizzle with hummus.
- Top with olives, tomato, cucumber, and cheese; bake in the preheated oven for about 4 minutes or until warmed through.
- Sprinkle with lemon zest and oregano and serve the nachos hot.

# Olive Hummus Spread

Total time: 10 minutes
Prep time: 10 minutes
Cook time: 0 minutes
Yield: 10 servings

## Ingredients
- 1 (7 ounces) container plain hummus
- 1 tbsp. Greek vinaigrette
- ½ cup pitted Kalamata olives, chopped
- 7 pita breads, each cut into 6 wedges

## Directions
- Spread the hummus on a serving plate.
- In a small bowl, mix vinaigrette and olives and spoon over the hummus.
- Serve with wedges of pita bread.

# Tuna Spread

Total time: 15 minutes
Prep time: 15 minutes
Cook time: 0 minutes
Yield: 16 servings

## Ingredients
- 1 shallot, chopped
- 1 (8 oz.) container cream cheese spread (chives-and-onion flavor)
- 1 tsp. Italian seasoning
- 1 hard-cooked egg, finely chopped
- 1 medium tomato, coarsely chopped
- 1 (6 oz.) can tuna, drained, cut into chunks
- ½ cup pitted Kalamata olives, halved
- 1 tbsp. chopped fresh parsley
- 48 crackers

## Directions
- Mix together shallot, cream cheese, and Italian seasoning in a small bowl until well blended; spread the mixture on a serving plate.
- Top with egg, tomato, tuna, olives, and parsley and serve with crackers.

# Mediterranean Salad Kabobs

Total time: 15 minutes
Prep time: 24 minutes
Cook time: 0 minutes
Yield: 24 servings

## Ingredients
- ¾ cup nonfat plain Greek yogurt
- 1 small clove garlic, chopped
- 2 tsp. chopped oregano leaves
- 2 tsp. chopped dill weed
- 2 tsp. raw honey
- ¼ tsp. sea salt

## Kabobs
- 12 slices English cucumber, halved crosswise
- 24 small grape tomatoes
- 24 pitted Kalamata olives
- 24 toothpicks

## Directions
- Mix the dip ingredients in a small bowl and set aside.
- Thread half slice cucumber, 1 tomato, and 1 olive on each cocktail pick.
- Serve the kabobs with dip.

# Mediterranean Nachos

Total time: 12 minutes
Prep time: 10 minutes
Cook time: 2 minutes
Yield: 6 servings

## Ingredients
- 2 tsp. oil from jar of sun-dried tomatoes
- 2 tbsp. chopped sun-dried tomatoes in oil
- 2 tbsp. chopped Kalamata olives
- 1 tbsp. chopped green onion
- 1 small plum tomato, finely chopped
- 30 restaurant-style corn tortilla chips
- 1 (4 oz.) package crumbled feta cheese

## Directions
- Mix together oil from the jar, sun-dried tomatoes, olives, onion, and plum tomato in a small bowl; set aside.
- Arrange the tortilla chips on a large microwavable plate and evenly top with cheese.
- Microwave on high for about 1 minute; rotate the plate and microwave for 1 minute more or until cheese is melted and bubbly.
- Evenly spoon the tomato mixture over the chips and cheese to serve.

# Roasted Beet Muhammara

Total time: 1 hour 20 minutes
Prep time: 20 minutes
Cook time: 1 hour
Yield: 1 ½ Cups

## Ingredients
- 9 oz. trimmed and rinsed red beets
- ¼ cup plus 1 tbsp. extra virgin olive oil, divided
- 1 ½ tsp. freshly squeezed lemon juice
- 1 ½ tbsp. pomegranate molasses
- ½ cup  sliced scallions
- 3/4 cup lightly toasted walnuts
- 1 tsp. ground cumin
- 1 tsp. Aleppo pepper
- Sea salt

## Directions
- Place a rack in the center of oven and preheat to 375°F.
- Place beets in a baking dish and rub with 1 tablespoon extra virgin olive oil and cover with foil.
- Roast in the preheated oven for about 1 hour or until tender.
- Remove from oven and let cool; peel and then chop to yield 1 cup.
- In a food processor, pulse together the beets, scallions, and walnuts until finely chopped.
- Add lemon juice, pomegranate molasses, cumin, pepper, ½ teaspoon sea salt and the remaining extra virgin olive oil; process until very smooth.
- Adjust seasoning to your liking and serve cold or at room temperature.

# Healthy Mediterranean Dip

Total time: 15 minutes
Prep time: 15 minutes
Cook time: 0 minutes
Yield: 8 servings

## Ingredients
- 1 can pineapple, drained
- ¼ cup coconut, flaked and toasted
- 16 strawberries
- 8 bunches grapes
- 2 nectarines, thinly sliced
- Choc chip cookies

## Directions
- Mix pineapple, coconut and yogurt in a bowl.
- Serve in 8 smaller bowls and top with fruit and cookies then cover and refrigerate for 1 hour.
- You are ready to eat!

# Mediterranean Salad Kabobs

Total time: 15 minutes
Prep time: 15 minutes
Cook time: 0 minutes
Yield: 24 servings

## Ingredients
- ¾ cup low fat plain Greek yogurt
- 2 tsp. fresh oregano, chopped
- 2 tsp. fresh dill weed, chopped
- 2 tsp. raw honey
- 1 small clove garlic, finely chopped
- ¼ tsp. sea salt
- 24 toothpicks
- 24 Kalamata olives, pitted
- 24 small grape tomatoes
- 3 English cucumbers, sliced and halved

## Directions
- Mix yogurt, oregano, dill, honey, garlic and salt in a bowl and set aside.
- Thread an olive, a tomato, half a slice of cucumber on each toothpick and serve with the dip.

# Roasted Veggie Hummus

Total time: 1 hour
Prep time: 20 minutes
Cook time: 40 minutes
Yield: 20 servings

## Ingredients
- 1 bulb garlic
- ¾ cup extra virgin olive oil, divided
- 1 eggplant, halved
- 1 red bell pepper, halved
- 2 cans chickpeas, drained
- ⅓ cup fresh lemon juice
- ¼ cup sesame tahini paste
- ⅓ tsp. smoked paprika
- ½ tsp. sea salt

## Directions
- Heat your oven to 450°F and line a baking pan with foil.
- Cut the very top of the garlic bulb off and drizzle with 1 tsp of olive oil.
- Next wrap it up in foil.
- On a separate pan, place the eggplant and bell pepper and drizzle with 2 tablespoons extra virgin olive oil and toss so it coats evenly.
- Place the wrapped garlic into the pan containing the vegetables.
- Roast for 30 minutes without covering and cool for 10 minutes.
- Remove the peels from eggplant and bell pepper and chop the vegetables into small pieces.
- Place the chickpeas in a food processor with a metal blade and process until smooth.
- Next, squeeze the pulp from the garlic into the processor; add all the other ingredients including the roasted vegetables and process until well blended.
- Spoon into small serving bowls and serve immediately.
- Refrigerate the remainder.

# Healthy Greek Dip

Total time: 25 minutes
Prep time: 25 minutes
Cook time: 0 minutes
Yield: 8 servings

## Ingredients
- ½ cup feta cheese, crumbled
- ½ a liter lemon yogurt
- 1 tsp. freshly squeezed lemon juice
- Sea salt, to taste
- 1 cup plain hummus
- ½ cup tomatoes, seeded and chopped
- ½ cup finely chopped English cucumber
- ½ cup Kalamata olives, pitted and chopped
- 2 tbsp. chopped green onions
- 1 tbsp. chopped fresh parsley

## Method
- Mix cheese, yogurt, lemon juice and salt in a small bowl.
- Line up 8 glasses and layer 2 tablespoons hummus, 1 teaspoon tomato, 1 tablespoon of yogurt mixture, 1 tablespoon of cucumber, I tablespoon olives and 1 teaspoon green onions.
- Top with the remaining ingredients.

# Mediterranean Salsa

Total time: 20 minutes
Prep time: 20 minutes
Cook time: 0 minutes
Yield: 6 servings

## Ingredients
- 1 cup zucchini, finely chopped
- 1 ½ cups tomatoes, seeded and chopped
- ½ cup roasted bell peppers, finely chopped
- 1 garlic clove, minced
- 1 ½ tsp. capers
- 1 tbsp. fresh flat leaf parsley, chopped
- 1 tbsp. fresh basil, chopped
- 2 tbsp. red onion, finely chopped
- 2 tsp. lemon juice
- 2 tsp. extra virgin olive oil
- A pinch of sea salt
- A pinch of black pepper, freshly ground

## Directions
Combine all ingredients in a bowl and serve immediately or refrigerate.

# Mediterranean Tapenade

Total time: 5 minutes
Prep time: 5 minutes
Cook time: 0 minutes
Yield: 8 servings

## Ingredients
- 1 cup Kalamata olives, pitted
- Juice of 1 lemon
- 2 tbsp. extra virgin olive oil
- 5 cloves garlic
- ¼ cup parsley, chopped
- 1 tbsp. capers
- ½ tsp. allspice

## Directions
- Place all the ingredients in a food processor and process until combined well.
- Serve in 8 small bowls.

# Mango Salsa

Total time: 20 minutes
Prep time: 20 minutes
Cook time: 0 minutes
Yield: 4 servings

## Ingredients
- 1 cup cucumber, chopped
- 2 cups mango, diced
- ½ cup cilantro, minced
- 2 tbsp. fresh lime juice
- 1 tbsp. scallions, minced
- ¼ tsp. chipotle powder
- ¼ tsp. sea salt

## Directions
Mix together all ingredients in a bowl and serve or refrigerate.

# Tzatziki

Total time: 26 minutes
Prep time: 20 minutes
Cook time: 6 minutes
Refrigerator time: At least 6 hours
Yield: 32 servings

## Ingredients
- 32 ounces plain Greek yogurt
- 5 cloves garlic, minced
- 1 English cucumber, peeled and grated
- ¼ cup olive oil
- 3 tbsp. distilled white vinegar
- Sea salt

## Directions
- Cover a medium bowl with a cheesecloth and strain the yogurt in the fridge for 6 hours or better still, overnight.
- Also drain as much water from the garlic and cucumber.
- Mix all the ingredients and stir until a thick mixture forms.

# Mediterranean Kale

Total time: 25 minutes
Prep time: 15 minutes
Cook time: 10 minutes
Yields: 6 servings

## Ingredients
- 12 cups chopped kale
- 1 tsp. soy sauce
- 1 tbsp. minced garlic
- 1 tbsp. olive oil or as needed
- 2 tbsp. lemon juice
- A pinch salt
- A pinch freshly ground black pepper

## Directions
- Add water to cover the bottom of a medium-sized saucepan; add steamer insert.
- Cover and bring the water to a boil.
- Add kale, cover and steam for about 10 minutes or until just tender.
- In a large bowl, whisk together soy sauce, garlic, olive oil, lemon juice, salt and pepper.
- Add the steamed kale to the bowl and toss until well coated.

# Mediterranean Desserts

## Spinach Cake

Total time: 1 hour
Prep time: 15 minutes
Cook time: 45 minutes
Yields: 12 Spinach Cakes

### Ingredients
- 1 ½ pounds spinach, rinsed
- 3 tbsp. extra virgin olive oil
- 1 cup pine nuts
- 2 cloves garlic, minced
- ½ cup currants
- 1 tsp. sea salt
- 2 large eggs, whisked

### Directions
- Wilt spinach in a pan set over low heat for about 5 minutes; drain and let cool a bit before squeezing moisture out of the spinach.
- Pulse the spinach in a food processor until coarsely chopped; set aside.
- Warm oil in a skillet; add pine nuts and sauté for a few minutes or until golden brown.
- Stir in garlic and continue cooking for 1 more minute.
- Combine the pine nut mixture, currants, blended spinach, eggs and salt in a bowl; spread the mixture into a coated baking dish and bake at 350°F for about 35 minutes.

# Citrus Tarts

Total time: 40 minutes
Prep time: 15 minutes
Cook time: 25 minutes
Yield: 6 servings

## Ingredients
- 1 ½ packs frozen mini phyllo pastry shells
- 1 cup whipping cream, divided
- ½ tsp. almond extract, divided
- ¼ cup orange curd
- ¼ cup strawberry curd
- Fresh mint leaves for garnish

## Directions
- Bake the pastry shells according to the package's instructions and set aside until they cool off completely.
- In a food processor, beat ½ cup whipping cream, ¼ teaspoon almond extract and orange curd until soft peaks start to form.
- Spoon this mixture into half the baked pastry shells.
- Again beat the remaining whipping cream, almond extract and strawberry curd in the food processor until soft peaks form and spoon in the remaining shells.
- Garnish with mint leaves and serve.

# Pistachio and Fruits

Total time: 12 minutes
Prep time: 5 minutes
Cook time: 7 minutes
Yield: 12 servings

## Ingredients
- 1 ¼ cups unsalted pistachios, roasted
- ½ cup apricots, dried and chopped
- ¼ cup dried cranberries
- ½ tsp. cinnamon
- 2 tsp. sugar
- ¼ tsp. allspice
- ¼ tsp. ground nutmeg

## Directions
- Preheat your oven to 350°F and bake pistachios in a baking tray for about 6 minutes.
- Set aside and let them cool completely.
- Mix all the ingredients in a bowl until well combined and you are ready to serve.

# Decorated Figs

Total time: 1 hour 10 minutes
Prep time: 15 minutes
Cook time: 40 minutes
Cooling time: 15 minutes
Yield: 6 servings

## Ingredients
- 1 cup dry red wine
- ½ cup sugar
- ½ cup balsamic vinegar
- 1 pound dried figs, remove stems
- ½ cup mascarpone
- ¾ cup toasted and chopped walnuts

## Directions
- Preheat oven to 350°F and place oven rack in mid position.
- Pour the wine, sugar and vinegar in a non-stick saucepan and bring to a boil over medium heat, stirring constantly until the sugar dissolves.
- Add figs to the pan and simmer for 5 minutes.
- Pour the contents of the saucepan into a ceramic baking dish and top with walnuts.
- Bake in preheated oven for about 30 minutes until the figs absorb most of the liquid.
- Set aside and let it cool for about 15 minutes then serve with the sauce and a generous topping of mascarpone.

# Grape Delight

Total time: 20 minutes
Prep time: 20 minutes
Cook time: 0 minutes
Refrigerator time: 1 hour
Yield: 8 servings

## Ingredients
- ¾ kg red seedless grapes, washed and drained
- ¾ kg green seedless grapes, washed and drained
- ¼ cup light cream cheese, softened
- ⅓ cup low-fat Greek yogurt
- 1 tsp. vanilla extract
- 2 tbsp. brown sugar
- ½ cup pecans, chopped
- ¼ cup sugar

## Directions
- Halve the grapes and set aside.
- Combine the cream cheese, yogurt, sugar and vanilla extract until well mixed.
- Add the grapes into the mixture and pour into a large serving dish
- In a separate dish, combine the brown sugar with the pecans and use this to top the grapes mixture completely.
- Refrigerate for at least an hour, then serve.

# Citrus, Honey and Cinnamon

Total time: 10 minutes
Prep time: 5 minutes
Cook time: 5 minutes
Yield: 4 servings

## Ingredients
- 4 oranges
- 2 tbsp. orange flower water
- 2 tbsp. raw honey
- 1 cinnamon stick
- 2 ½ tbsp. toasted and sliced walnuts

## Directions
- Peel the oranges and slice them thinly in round shapes.
- Arrange the oranges on a bowl.
- Meanwhile, in a small, heavy saucepan, combine orange flower water, honey and cinnamon stick.
- Stir gently over low heat until the mixture starts simmering, about 2 minutes.
- Pour the hot liquid on the oranges and let it cool, then top with walnuts.
- Best served when cold.

# Sweet Cherries

Total time: 2 hours, 10 minutes
Cook time: 10 minutes
Refrigerator time: 2 hours
Yield: 4 servings

## Ingredients
- ½ kg fresh cherries, washed and pitted
- 2 cups of water
- ¾ cup sugar
- 15 peppercorns
- 1 small vanilla bean, split
- 3 strips orange zest
- 3 strips lemon zest

## Directions
- Set cherries aside.
- Add rest of ingredients to a saucepan and bring to a boil, stirring constantly until all the sugar is dissolved.
- Now, add the cherries and simmer for about 10 minutes until soft but not disintegrated.
- Pour out the foam on the surface and set aside to cool.
- Put in the fridge for about 2 hours.
- Strain the liquid before serving.
- Best enjoyed when served with ice cream.

# Summer Delight

Total time: 2 hours 10 minutes
Prep time: 2 hour 10 minutes
Cook time: 0 minutes
Yield: 3 servings

## Ingredients
- ⅓ kg peaches, sliced
- 2 tbsp. freshly squeezed lemon juice
- ½ bottle of sweet red wine
- 1 tbsp. brown sugar

## Directions
- Dip the peach slices in lemon to prevent oxidation.
- Pour the wine in a bowl and add sugar to it, then pour in the peaches together with their juice.
- Cover the bowl and refrigerate for at least 2 hours.
- Serve cold.

# Sweetened Roasted Figs

Total time: 1 hour
Prep time: 5 minutes
Cook time: 30 minutes
Refrigerator time: 1 hour
Yield: 4 servings

## Ingredients
- 12 ripe figs
- ½ cup sugar
- Ricotta cheese

## Directions
- Preheat your oven to 450°F and arrange figs on a baking dish standing upright.
- Meanwhile spread sugar on a skillet and place on low heat.
- Shake the skillet to distribute the sugar when it starts melting.
- Continue doing this until all the sugar melts, about 15 minutes.
- Pour caramel over figs.
- Now roast the figs in the caramel for 15 minutes and set aside to cool.
- Refrigerate the figs for an hour.
- Arrange the figs on plates and drizzle with the caramel.
- Top with the ricotta cheese.

# Fig Ice Cream

Total time: 1 hour
Prep time: 15 minutes
Cook time: 45 minutes
Yield: 4 servings

## Ingredients
- ½ cup ripe figs, stems removed
- ⅓ cup sugar, plus 2 tbsp. sugar
- ⅓ cup honey
- 2 cups half-and-half
- 1 tsp. anise seed
- 3 eggs, separated
- 1 cup crème fraiche

## Directions
- Place the figs in a food processor and process until it forms a puree and transfer this to a skillet containing ⅓ cup sugar.
- Cook over medium heat, stirring constantly so that it doesn't stick, for about 30 minutes until it forms a sort of jam.
- In a separate saucepan, heat the honey, half-and-half, and anise seed and bring to a boil. Stir constantly until the honey dissolves.
- Whisk a bit of the hot cream into the egg yolks, pour them into the pan, and continue stirring until the mixture thickens and coats the spoon.
- Transfer this to a bowl and pour in the fig mixture and crème fraiche and chill.
- Whisk the egg whites together with the remaining 2 tbsp. sugar until soft peaks form.
- Fold this into the fig mixture and put in an ice cream maker, following the instructions of the ice cream maker.
- Serve when ready.

# Mediterranean Smoothies

## Skinny Smoothie

Total time: 5 minutes
Yields: 2 servings

### Ingredients
- ½ cup freshly squeezed tangerine or orange juice
- ½ cup honeydew chunks
- ½ banana, chopped
- 1 kiwi, peeled and thinly chopped
- ½ cup frozen non-fat plain Greek yogurt or frozen kefir
- 1 cup baby spinach
- ¼ cup fresh mint leaves, plus extra sprigs for garnish

### Directions
- Combine everything in a blender and blend until smooth and creamy.
- Serve in two tall glasses and garnish with a mint sprig.

## Mango Smoothie Surprise

Total time: 5 minutes
Yields: 1 serving

### Ingredients
- 1 tbsp. lime juice (freshly squeezed)
- ¼ cup nonfat vanilla yogurt
- ½ cup fresh mango juice
- ¼ cup mashed avocado
- ¼ cup diced mango
- ½ tbsp. honey
- 6 ice cubes

### Directions
- Combine all the ingredients in a blender and blend on high until smooth.
- Pour in a tall serving glass and garnish with a strawberry or mango slice, if desired. Enjoy!

# Pumpkin Smoothie

Total time: 15 minutes
Yield: 2 servings

## Ingredients
- ½ cup skim milk
- ½ cup ice, crushed
- ½ cup pumpkin butter
- ⅓ cup of low-fat Greek yogurt
- 2 tsps. maple syrup
- ½ tsp. cinnamon
- 2 tsp. vanilla extract

## Directions
Combine all ingredients in a blender and blend until smooth.
Serve in a tall glass with a straw.

# Oat-Berry Smoothie

Total time: 5 minutes
Yields: 2 servings

## Ingredients
- ½ cup oats
- 1 cup nonfat plan Greek yogurt
- 1 cup unsweetened almond milk
- ½ banana
- ½ cup berries

## Directions
Combine all ingredients in a blender and blend until very smooth.
Enjoy!

# Banana Blueberry Blast

Total time: 5 minutes
Yields: 2 servings

## Ingredients
- 1 ½ cups plain nonfat Greek yogurt
- 1 cup blueberries
- 1 banana
- 5 walnuts
- ½ cup oats

## Directions
Add all the ingredients to a blender and blend until very smooth. Enjoy!


# Berry Bliss

Total time: 5 minutes
Yields: 2 servings

## Ingredients:
- 2 cups plain low-fat Greek yogurt
- 1 tbsp. flaxseed
- 2 tbsp. almond butter
- 1 cup frozen blueberries
- 1 cup frozen strawberries
- 1 frozen banana

## Directions:
Combine all ingredients in a blender and blend until smooth.

# Parting Shot

It's common knowledge that people in countries in the Mediterranean region live longer and suffer less, than most people across the globe, from chronic illnesses such as heart diseases, cancer, and type 2 diabetes. The Mediterranean diet is an active lifestyle that involves eating fresh, healthy, and natural ingredients.

Of all the basic tenets in life, health and nutrition rank first. Your first priority should always be to provide your body with quality nutrition—and what better way than the Mediterranean diet?

If you have tried a thousand ways to lose weight without success, this is your best time to start. If you do this, by the same time next week, you will be several pounds lighter, thanks to this amazing diet—and week after week you will be a healthier and lighter version of who you are now.

The tasty recipes in this book will help place healthy food in the heart of your home, and they will help you have great family fun time during meals.

Feel free to tweak the recipes and substitute certain ingredients with your favorite ones to make your very own signature dish.

All the best as you embark on your health journey and I wish you great health and motivation as you seek to find health and joy with the help of the Mediterranean diet.

Made in the USA
San Bernardino, CA
27 October 2016